Elite • 151

World War II Jungle Warfare Tactics

Dr Stephen Bull · Illustrated by Steve Noon

Consultant editor Martin Windrow

First published in Great Britain in 2007 by Osprey Publishing,
Midland House, West Way, Botley, Oxford OX2 0PH, UK
443 Park Avenue South, New York, NY 10016, USA

Email: info@ospreypublishing.com

ISBN 978 1 84603 069 7

Editor: Martin Windrow
Page layouts by Ken Vail Graphic Design, Cambridge, UK
Typeset in Helvetica Neue and ITC New Baskerville
Index by Alan Thatcher
Originated by PPS Grasmere, Leeds, UK
Printed in China through World Print Ltd.

07 08 09 10 11   10 9 8 7 6 5 4 3 2 1

A CIP catalogue record for this book is available from the British Library

FOR A CATALOGUE OF ALL BOOKS PUBLISHED BY OSPREY MILITARY AND
AVIATION PLEASE CONTACT:

North America:
Osprey Direct
C/o Random House Distribution Centre, 400 Hahn Road, Westminster,
MD 21157, USA
Email: info@ospreydirect.com

All other regions:
Osprey Direct UK
PO Box 140, Wellingborough, Northants NN8 2FA, UK
Email: info@ospreydirect.co.uk

Buy online at www.ospreypublishing.com

Author's Note

For reasons of space, basic infantry tactics are not
described in this text, but only their adaption to jungle
conditions. Readers are recommended to the titles listed
on the inside back cover, particularly Elites 105 and 122
and Warrior 95.

Acknowledgements

A number of people have helped make this book possible.
Particular thanks are due to Gary Smith, Curator, King's
Liverpools, and latterly Manchester Regiment; Jane Davies,
Queen's Lancashire Regiment, for her help with manuals
and photographs; David Hopkins, Imperial War Museum;
jungle instructor Richmond Dutton, and Captain Teddy
Dickson. Former housemate Toshio Maruka provided
valuable insights into things Japanese. Practical experience
of jungle would have been lacking were it not for 'Mad Mac'
Macleod and our guides in Laos, Jit and Kan. I trust that my
copious use of a wide range of anti-malarial precautions,
and steadfast refusal to remove my boots (unless sharing
them with wildlife), continues to give them amusement.

Artist's Note

Readers may care to note that the original paintings from
which the colour plates in this book were prepared are
available for private sale. All reproduction copyright
whatsoever is retained by the Publishers. All enquiries
should be addressed to:

Steve Noon,
50 Colchester Avenue,
Penylan,
Cardiff CF23 9BP,
Wales,
UK
hi.noon@virgin.net

The Publishers regret that they can enter into no
correspondence upon this matter.

Editor's Note

The frequent quotations from 1940s documents of both
British and US origin, and the modern spelling conventions
used in the narrative, have inevitably resulted in a number of
inconsistencies in this text. It is hoped that readers will not
find these distracting.

WORLD WAR II JUNGLE WARFARE TACTICS

INTRODUCTION

'The night sounds in the jungle comprise a cacophony of strange and eerie grunts, groans, whistles, hisses, catcalls, growls and coughs, from every sort of animal which takes the opportunity of the night to replenish its stomach and perform its natural functions. To pick out from all these sounds the approach of the enemy took a lot of listening, looking and smelling, for all the senses had to be alerted.'

These first impressions of Capt Peter Grant of the Cameron Highlanders in 1944 are not untypical. Even today, experienced travellers resort to earplugs to get to sleep; and by daylight the jungle remains alive with the strangely electronic noises of insects, lizards, and the calls of primates. Charles Walker, with the US 164th Infantry, claimed that his comrades could quite literally smell the enemy – a sweetish odour of leather equipment and perspiration. While sounds and smells seem amplified, visibility is severely limited – sometimes to little more than arm's length.

Initial responses may include claustrophobia, and terror of the unknown. For Maj Bernard Fergusson the jungle soon became what he described as 'a place of stealth, a place in which to wage war, a place which affords cover to approach your enemy, and for him to stalk you'.

General Frank Messervy, commander of 7th Indian Div, felt that fear of the jungle was, in part, a feeling that 'you were being watched all the time' – his men spoke in whispers, and often slept with a wire tied to a toe, by which they could be woken quietly at the first sign of danger.

Yet 'jungle' is by no means all of a piece. The apparently uniform wild green blanket of South-East Asia is richly varied, and – perhaps surprisingly – even in 1941 significant portions of it were landscaped by human activity. Only 'primary' jungle – known in Australia as 'high' jungle, with its mature trees and lofty canopy – is truly natural. On his first visit to the Malayan jungle Col Spencer Chapman was astonished to see the perfectly straight and symmetrical tree trunks rising 'like the pillars of a dark and limitless cathedral. The ground itself was covered with a thick carpet of dead leaves and seedling trees. There was practically no earth visible and certainly no grass or flowers.' Next to the great tree trunks the most remarkable thing was the amount of parasitic growth – creepers, vines, mosses and ferns, many of which actually hung in the air between the treetops.

Oddly, this genuine jungle of half-light and deep shadows can sometimes be crossed without too much

Lt W.K. Fussell, Royal Corps of Signals, Far East, 1945. In jungle terrain, with its problems of observation, the signallers often had to be well up with the leading infantry, despite the difficulty of moving and maintaining bulky and often fragile equipment. Note the 1944 pattern short-brim bush hat and uniform in jungle-green, developed after the research tour of British and Allied units in the Far East by MajGen J.S. Lethbridge's mission between October 1943 and March 1944. Even Lt Fussell's spectacles are of special military design, with flexible side frames allowing them to be worn under the respirator (gasmask).

An example of tropical topography, as seen from a track in northern Laos, 2005, but typical of SE Asia in 1941–45. Here a stick fence is used to keep animals, wild and domestic, out of the modest patch of plantation. Beyond the cultivation, thick secondary or low jungle has begun to grow back; and on the steep slopes in the background can be seen the tall trees of primary or high jungle, with its distinctive canopy.

difficulty. Where the original forest has been cleared, perhaps by logging or the primordial slash-and-burn cultivation of native peoples, 'secondary' or 'low' jungle grows back. With no tall trees to blot out the sunlight, bamboo, thorn thickets and underbrush mesh together in such a way that any path has to be cut laboriously through its depths. A third form of jungle, characterized by more open spaces, girded many of the coastal areas; here the obstacles to vision and movement were mainly mangrove swamps and tall grasses.

In some areas, during the dry season, jungle is more brown than green – dusty, wreathed in the smoke from burning scrub, and carpeted with dead leaves and bamboo which crackles loudly underfoot. Paddy fields, a morass when wet, may dry out to the consistency of concrete, and the main obstacle to travel then becomes the water-retaining *bunds* or banks around their margins.

More often, however, jungle is wet – or more accurately, humid. Pfc James Jones of the US 25th Div on Guadalcanal – later to fictionalize his experience in *The Thin Red Line* – described such humidity as so great that it was more like 'a material object than a weather condition'. When heat and wet are combined the processes of growth and decomposition are accelerated. As foliage grows quickly, so leather equipment, fabric, even books and paper deteriorate surprisingly fast. In the human context, sores, scratches and insect bites stubbornly fail to heal, and fungal infections are rife. As one jungle warfare instructor put it with brutal simplicity, 'you rot'.

Movement and navigation

At the outbreak of World War II in the East there were large areas of Malaya, Burma, Thailand, the Dutch East Indies and the Pacific islands which were not covered with true jungle at all, but had been tamed to make way for plantations of rubber, bananas, pineapples and other crops. Sometimes these were laid out on an industrial scale, but more often they formed small and not always obvious 'native gardens'. While often impassable to vehicles, and far from open, most plantations could be traversed quite easily on foot. Few jungles were genuinely 'impenetrable', in fact, and it is a myth that they were believed to be so in 1941. British theorists had published treatises on fighting in jungle as early as the 19th century, and Maj Gordon Casserly's *Manual of Training for Jungle and River Warfare* appeared in 1914. An official volume entitled *Notes on Training in Bush and Jungle Warfare* was produced in 1922, with an amended version in 1930. In the popular imagination, jungles are always crossed only with sweat and sharp machetes; but in World War II, as now, this was the method of last resort.

What the Japanese referred to as a 'chopping group' was expected to maintain a speed of just a quarter of a mile per hour, with a maximum distance of four to six miles per day being achieved in good conditions. The much-praised performance of the Japanese 42nd Inf Regt through the 'inferno of heat' in the jungle at Kampar, Malaya, saw them manage just three miles in three days. US training literature stated that a trained man was capable of clearing '100 square yards of trail' in five hours. Where there were insufficient fresh men to rotate to the head of the march, or in bad weather or

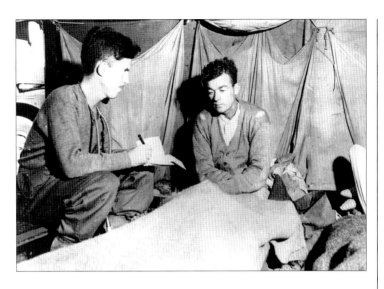

under enemy interference, the daily rate of advance might be measured in hundreds of yards rather than miles. Lieutenant John Randle of the 7/10th Baluchis described the whole process as 'useless', not merely on grounds of lack of progress but because it was so exhausting and noisy.

In most instances motor vehicles were channelled on to the few viable roads, or boats were used to travel along jungle waterways. Where road and river ran out, faint native trails still linked settlements and plantations. When all sign of human presence had been left behind, walking along streambeds was the natural recourse – leeches being the main hazard of this method. Yet jungle navigation is rarely simple: as Maj Fergusson explained, one is 'submerged' in the jungle, and to reach a hill with a view is like suddenly emerging from a deck hatch on a boat. Other metaphors occurred to the Japanese: Ogawa Masatsugu thought of New Guinea as a 'desert of green… full of greenness, all year long'. The problem is not merely lack of landmarks. With rotation of crops, jungle becomes plantation, and plantation jungle, from year to year. In some places jungle dwellers also abandon their villages at intervals, and build afresh. New settlements may keep the old names, or be distinguished by the addition of a suffix meaning, for example, 'north' or 'new'.

The jungle as battlefield

Under these conditions, only one arm of service was truly suited to jungle warfare. As the US manual *Jungle Warfare* tersely explained: 'Jungle fighting is performed largely by infantry. Combat is usually characterised by close fighting. Support of infantry by other arms will frequently be impractical or impossible.'

As infantry did most of the fighting, so they also did most of the dying. One example suffices to illustrate the point. During 1944 in Burma the 26th Indian ('Tiger Head') Div suffered a total of 2,255 battle casualties, of which about a quarter were fatalities. Just over 93 per cent of these fell to the infantry; 3 per cent were artillerymen; just under 1 per cent were engineers, and the remaining 3 per cent were distributed between the medics, signallers, headquarters, Royal Indian Army Service Corps and others.

Battle fatigue: a British soldier is interviewed by a doctor of 154th Field Ambulance, RAMC, in Burma. Apart from the strain of repeated close combat, often with little warning, the climate and the terrain were exhausting for Western and Japanese troops alike. The high humidity led to distressing skin diseases; cuts and sores refused to heal; and there was a constant risk of catching malaria, which was seriously debilitating. Once a man was infected, attacks could recur intermittently for months or years, as new generations of parasites hatched from the victim's liver. The mosquito may not have killed as efficiently as the Japanese, but on several fronts – and notably in Burma – it put many more men out of action than the enemy's fire. In 1943, roughly half the British and Indian troops serving there received some form of hospital treatment for the disease. (Queen's Lancashire Regiment)

War in the twilight: in 1944 a Gurkha from 36th Div, photographed in the 'Railway Corridor' area of Burma between Myitkyina and Katha on the Irrawaddy, demonstrates how effectively bamboo and simple camouflage could conceal the human form. (QLR)

Jungle imposed three major limitations upon the infantry that fought there in 1941–45. The first – lack of visibility and fields of fire – necessitated drastic revisions of small unit tactics. The second – remoteness, and obstruction to transport – not only influenced the way troops fought in battle, in ambush and on patrol, but imposed sometimes insurmountable problems on supply and the movement of heavy equipment. Getting the simplest things to the soldier could be extremely difficult: Gen Slim cited specific problems with milk, rotting cartons and rusting tins. Japanese food packaging was inadequate early in the war, and their transport almost non-existent at the end.

The third governing condition was the tropical climate itself; humidity combined with insect life and stagnant water to produce a bewildering variety of diseases, many of them unknown in Europe. Whilst cholera and typhus were killers, it was debilitating fevers, and above all malaria, that cut a swathe through the ranks of those who fought in the jungle. Malaria, caused by a parasite injected while the mosquito sucked a man's blood, came in several forms, attacking in cycles of one, two or three days. Its onset was rapid, as Maj David Atkins recorded:

'The speed and fierceness of malaria was extraordinary to see. It comes on much faster than influenza and gives a higher temperature. At first a man feels hot and flushed and the temperature rises to 104 degrees. When the fever breaks the man sweats profusely. Then, even if he is being bumped up and down in the back of a lorry and with no pillow, he seems to recover quickly and is soon quite lucid, although very limp.'

To a large extent, jungle warfare in World War II is the story of how Allied forces not only confronted and overcame the Japanese with new tactics and weapons, but how they successfully adapted to natural factors – understanding that far from being a friend to the enemy, 'the jungle is neutral'.

ALLIED FAILURE, 1941–42

British Empire forces

It is often stated that the Japanese triumphs of late 1941 and early 1942 came about because they were better 'jungle trained' than Allied forces. British documents seeking to explain the disaster at Singapore speak of 'the fact' that the Japanese, 'being seasoned veterans, were better trained for jungle warfare'. This was, at best, a gross oversimplification.

In reality the British forces in SE Asia were a very mixed 'Imperial Force'. Indian troops predominated, making up half or more of the total infantry strength. The Indian Army was not a homogeneous body: many languages were spoken, and although the many historical and cultural traditions were held together by loyalty to regimental officers and the Crown, morale in some units was undermined by nationalist unrest at home. Considerations of caste were sometimes opposed to those of rank. One of the most scathing critics would be Gen Orde Wingate, who compared the Indian Army to a well-organized 'system for outdoor relief' – that is, more useful as an employer of the poor than as a modern military force. Battle training concentrated on fitting units to fight tribal enemies in the harsh but open terrain of the rocky Indian North-West Frontier. After much debate a programme of motorization of the Indian Army had been begun, but with an eye to hills and plains rather than jungle. As one recent historian of the Gurkhas has observed, Indian battalions were unwittingly trained for 'the wrong sort of war'. The history of the 10th Gurkha Rifles actually records that the unit was very disappointed when it was stationed in Shillong, where there was a good deal of jungle, since this was viewed as totally unsuitable for training.

The Indian Army's infantry weapons remained old-fashioned. Indian forces officially adopted the Vickers Berthier light machine gun in 1933, but in many units the elderly Lewis gun survived until 1936. Infantry mortars were slow to materialize, and practice was infrequent. Indian factories would continue to produce the Great War SMLE rifle long after Britain had introduced the No.4. Sub-machine guns of any description would remain a rarity until after the early Japanese victories.

In 1938 Gen Auchinleck, Deputy Chief of the General Staff/India, had uttered the depressing opinion that the Indian Army was 'unfit to take the field' against a modern enemy, and it is little wonder that the Indian Army's objectives at the outbreak of war were limited. As reported in *War*, the bulletin of the Army Bureau of Current Affairs, these were: the defence of India's frontiers; the maintenance of internal security; and lastly, 'the provision of certain land forces equivalent to a division, for the external defence of India'. After September 1939 things deteriorated further, as the skill levels in Indian formations in the Far East were diluted by massive recruitment, and they were simultaneously 'milked' of their best officers and junior leaders. Seasoned troops were

Before the outbreak of war in the Far East, jungle training for British troops was not unheard of; but it had a low priority, and was fatally belated in Malaya in 1941, when most of the troops' time was spent digging fortifications. Here, men of the 2nd Bn Argyll & Sutherland Highlanders emerge from a plantation during jungle training, and march back to barracks led by their pipes; on one occasion the battalion caused some astonishment by making a march of 60 miles in three days. The 2nd Argylls' CO, Maj Ian Stewart, was unusual in his insistence on such training, and was regarded as a crank by less energetic officers; after the British defeats, higher command became much more interested in his ideas and experience. See Plate A1 for details of the KD uniform and sun helmet. (Imperial War Museum 180171)

earmarked for active operations in North Africa and the Middle East (where they would make a notable contribution); Brig Key of 8th Indian Bde was typical in complaining that each of his battalions had lost an average of 240 of its best men, these being replaced by young recruits whose main training had been the firing of 50 rounds on the range.

Providing for the Indian Army in Malaya and Burma proved especially difficult; different religions required different types of meat, and some none at all. Tinned meat found favour with none, and *ghee* and milk which might have made up for deficiencies were less easy to provide. The bulk of the supplies were gathered in north-western India on the premise that they would be most likely to be needed there, or in the Middle East; and, like the infantry, transport units were rapidly expanded with inexperienced men. Major David Atkins noted that his own 309th General Purposes Transport Company was hastily filled up with 400 other ranks speaking six different languages – notionally divided into two Malayali, one Tamil and one Telegu platoon. Few could actually drive, and there was time for only the most rudimentary tuition before the arrival of Ford 3-ton lorries from Canada. As Atkins recorded:

'We tried our lorries the next morning and they were real pigs. The weight was half on the front wheels and so the steering was very heavy indeed. The driver sat high in the air and had great difficulty in judging how the lorries turned. By now most of the men had had twenty hours of road driving each, but that had been on a flat plain in convoy in a car, and it was all they had ever done in their lives. They had no experience of ordinary traffic.'

On the eve of the Japanese attack in December 1941, the key combat formations defending Malaya were 9th and 11th Indian Divs – motorized for desert warfare. Whilst British propaganda films talked about 'fortress Singapore', and the relative ease of ambushing the enemy using the jungle skills of local Malay volunteers, the performance of columns of vehicles driven by raw recruits on narrow tracks should have been predictable. Just one of the scenes of chaos was witnessed by LtCol S.D'Aubuz of 88th Field Regt, Royal Artillery, just prior to the battle at Gurun in northern Malaya:

'Trouble arose early in that, at about 0030 hours, the first of an uncoordinated rabble of Indian drivers started to arrive at both entrances to the camp, and, disregarding traffic policemen, effectively blocked both exits and prevented the regiment from marching. It took three quarters of an hour and many threats, including the use of the revolver, to clear a passage to let the regiment through.'

On the Burma front the experience of the 309th GPTC would be just as bad. Roads turned to mud, and on single-track mountain roads lorries slithered off or broke down, blocking the trail until they could be pushed aside. On narrow jungle tracks an average speed of 10mph was good for

A propaganda photo of a Japanese infantryman posing with his Arisaka 6.5mm Type 38 rifle; dating back to 1905, this was a basic, robust, bolt-action weapon of Mauser type with a five-round fixed magazine. The fixed bayonet is often seen in photos of Japanese troops, and the bayonet charge continued to feature significantly in Japanese tactics until 1945. Prisoners were routinely used for bayonet practice – new arrivals with an IJA unit were ordered to kill them as an initiation. This soldier wears the Type 90 woollen uniform used in China. (IWM HU72213)

heavy lorries: if the mission was complicated by bad weather and steep gradients, a steady walking speed was the best that could be expected.

To make matters worse, air superiority over Malaya was lost very early on, and columns of vehicles, transport nodes and ferries became prime targets for Japanese aircraft. As Gen Bill Slim would observe, with benefit of hindsight, the British were trapped by their 'tin can' of mechanical transport, while the Japanese were able to turn their weakness in motor vehicles into strength. In Burma similar tactical problems would be compounded by initial weakness and the intervention of the anti-British Burma Independence Army – though here at least the retreating forces had somewhere to escape to, falling back rapidly in the direction of India.

* * *

It would be grossly unfair to suggest that failure was solely due to Indian Army establishments, or to the performance of the rank and file. The expectations of British staff officers in the Far East were wide of the mark; there was a widespread underestimation of the Japanese, and an antiquated approach to training and equipment. Recent research by Tim Moreman, Alan Jeffreys and others suggests that a short pamphlet entitled *Notes on Forest Warfare* was produced by the Military Training Directorate of GHQ India in 1940, but that it failed to get beyond Command Headquarters in Malaya. A rather simplistic volume entitled *Tactical Notes for Malaya* did actually get circulated, but had little practical impact. It is therefore unlikely that many of the infantry received tactical instruction beyond that given in the 1937 *Infantry Training*, and the 1938 *Infantry Section Leading*. Much of what these contained was designed for temperate and relatively open battlefields – and the little that they did have on 'bush fighting' left a lot to be desired. *Infantry Section Leading*, for example, was keen to point out that columns advancing through thick woods were likely to be ambushed, but offered no idea of what to do in this eventuality, beyond suggesting that the opposition should be 'rushed', especially if they were 'uncivilized enemies'. On navigation, it was remarked that maintaining direction required 'constant attention', but that 'men experienced in wood and bush craft develop an instinct for keeping direction'.

Officers keen to find out more about soldiering in the Far East on their own account had plenty of literature to consult, but much of it was either useless or at least outdated. An example of this genre was the well-meaning but often farcical *Tropical Tips for Troops*, published by LtCol E.T.Burke in 1941. Here the aspiring officer learned of the vital importance of a thick tropical pith helmet; before leaving the UK one was advised to get

Japanese tactics for a battalion night attack (up the page), when the objectives were usually less ambitious than during daylight, although the attack would be preceded by a period of infiltration to neutralize the enemy response. Two companies are tasked with seizing the first objective, the fresh third and fourth companies passing through them. Individual platoons within the companies remain in loose columns unless resistance dictates otherwise, and one platoon is kept back as reserve. (From the US *Handbook on Japanese Military Forces*)

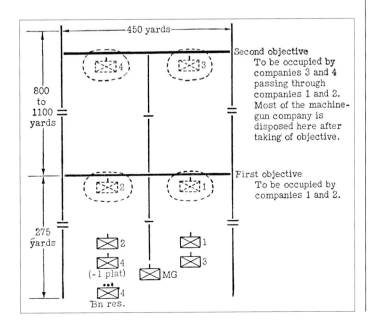

'some obliging girlfriend' to run up a 'bell shaped structure' of mosquito net to fit over it. For very hot weather Burke recommended a spine pad – a thick piece of khaki material worn down the middle of the back and buttoned to the shirt or tunic. In bed, or 'whilst taking a siesta', a woollen 'cholera belt' was essential; at need, one might be improvised by 'wrapping a puttee around your waist and abdomen'. Three pairs of sunglasses, a flywhisk, fly swatter, and warm woollen pyjamas for mountain areas were also recommended. While *Tropical Tips* gave no advice on actual fighting, it did urge on the novice the importance of keeping up the 'decencies of civilised life' and avoiding 'going native'. Burke was no teetotaller, but gave a stern warning against degenerating into 'a physically unclean gin-sodden wreck for whom the native has nothing but the most profound contempt'. Water was to be drunk sparingly, if at all, during the day. In short, adaptation to the environment was positively to be avoided, as was getting close enough to the locals to learn anything.

However, while tactical training for jungle warfare was conspicuous mainly by its absence, there were pockets of skill amongst British Empire forces even in 1941. An example commonly cited is 2nd Bn Argyll & Sutherland Highlanders, whose commanding officer was actually ridiculed for his persistence in taking his men into the jungle, and who were nicknamed the 'Jungle Beasts' for their efforts. Despite Maj Ian Stewart's tireless work, postings and upheavals ensured that only a portion of his battalion received detailed instruction. Though little account had so far been taken of their presence, there were also skilled jungle practitioners amongst the men of the Assam Rifles and units of the Royal West African Frontier Force.

The 8th Australian Div embarked on jungle training as soon as it arrived in theatre. Particular claims have been made on behalf of Maj C.G.W.Anderson and his 2/19th Bn, who were said to have achieved an early 'moral ascendancy' over the enemy by means of bushcraft and fire control, succeeding in taking advantage of the Japanese infantry's tendency to bunch together during their attacks. Any success was fleeting, however, and the Australians buckled just like their British and Indian comrades when the enemy forced their way on to Singapore Island.

United States forces

Remarkably, the US Army also had a tradition of jungle warfare that stretched back to the 19th century and the Santiago campaign of 1898. In 1916 a detachment conducted a trek across the Panama Isthmus, and later the Panama Mobile Force became the main centre for American knowledge. Jungle warfare would also be touched upon by the Infantry School at Fort Benning, with a brief summary of its teaching receiving a relatively limited circulation in its *Infantry School Mailing List* publication of July 1936.

Although detailed tactics were as yet lacking, there was a clear realization that 'Jungle terrain, because of its low visibility, poor means of communication, and difficulties of movement and control, is conducive to the organised action of small units only. Hence jungle combat training should stress decentralisation by commanders and initiative to subordinates'. Large forces were seen as seriously impaired under jungle conditions, since 'not more than one or two of the leading squads of each column can fight' on a jungle trail.

To move through thicker vegetation, experience in trail-cutting was seen as a necessity, with multiple trails making flanking manoeuvre possible. For trail-cutting the bayonet was hopeless, and it was therefore recommended that 'bolos, machetes, or other large knives should be provided for this purpose. The heavy issue bolo is unsatisfactory... The Panamanian machete, the best type of jungle cutting tool, is on the order of a long butcher knife, a little heavier and somewhat narrower... nearest the handle'. Interestingly, the machine gun, 37mm infantry gun and mortars were all largely dismissed as jungle warfare weapons at this date, preference being given to rifle and bayonet.

At the time of Pearl Harbor the US Army possessed no basic field manual on jungle warfare. FM 31-20 *Jungle Warfare* was released belatedly on 15 December: this was useful, though not particularly relevant, since it was based on experience of jungles in the Western hemisphere. Nevertheless, there had been progress since 1936, and a wider range of infantry weapons were now recommended, with the emphasis on 'short range arms easily supplied with ammunition and readily transported over difficult terrain'. The primary arms were therefore the rifle and bayonet, automatic rifle, pistol, sub-machine gun, hand grenade and machete. The light machine gun and 60mm mortar could be regarded as 'secondary' weapons, while the heavy machine gun and 81mm would probably see use only where water or animal transport were available. Ammunition supply might well prove crucial. As FM 31-20 observed:

'The pistol and submachine gun have the great advantage of using the same type of lightweight ammunition. The bayonet and grenade are the true infantry weapons of close combat, although the grenade is too heavy and bulky for transport in quantity. The machete, a tool indispensable to the jungle soldier, is also an excellent weapon for close combat.'

Japanese infantry during their victorious advance in Malaya, 1941–42; for the Southern Army deployed to SE Asia much lighter, looser clothing was issued than in China. The foreground soldier wears the typical field cap with cloth-strip neck flap, cotton shirt and half-breeches, puttees, and canvas-and-rubber *tabi* boots with divided toes. The British Lt Bob Sutcliffe of 137th Field Regt RA described his captors' dress as 'simple, untidy and efficient... Webbing is not worn, but a leather belt to which stout leather rectangular ammunition boxes are attached; in the belt is invariably hooked also a sweat cloth, a bayonet, and a [captured, cylindrical, 50-size] Capstan cigarette tin suspended by a piece of string'. The IJA also paid attention to special items for jungle terrain: spiked 'crampons' were issued for tree-climbing, and caped camouflage cloaks were made from local foliage, patterned on the traditional rice-straw rain cape of the Japanese peasant.

In the attack, US commanders were warned that the 'determined execution' of a pre-arranged plan was crucial to success, since there would be little chance to make changes later. Envelopment tactics were thought likely to be even more effective – and psychologically powerful – in jungle than in open terrain. Since maintaining linear formations was generally impossible, and control was difficult, advances were usually conducted in files – squad columns for forward elements, platoon columns for those further from the enemy. On contact the best reaction was offensive, with scouts and patrols attempting to overcome the enemy advance detachments with 'the least possible noise or disturbance. When resistance is encountered which the scouts and patrols cannot overcome, the assault units deploy and both by frontal attack and manoeuvre seek to dislodge and destroy the hostile elements.' As jungle combat was prone to develop into many small independent actions, the 'initiative and troop leading ability of lower commanders are of major importance'.

Defence was also recognized as difficult, since vegetation could conceal the attacker and limited the co-ordination of defending fire. Where to defend was not obvious, since it was not always clear what points would impede the enemy, but the ideal position would 'offer such a threat to a hostile advance as to require its reduction'. High ground, located behind natural obstacles such as rivers, gorges or unusually thick jungle, was the optimum. Individual defensive positions were to be close, so as to cope with the lack of visibility and support weapons. Clearing proper fields of fire for automatic weapons was not always practicable, but often it would be possible to cut flanking 'lanes' which the enemy would struggle to cross. Trimming only the lower branches of trees would leave much of the jungle canopy intact, thereby hampering aerial observation. Even so, it is apparent that the US theorists of 1941 were still thinking primarily in terms of front lines rather than all-round defence, believing that secure flanks were of supreme importance.

* * *

In the event, the 1941 manual would have little impact in the limited time before the small US forces were ejected from the Philippines. Despite episodes of heroism, such as the annihilation of a whole Japanese battalion on Bataan in January 1942, US troops would fare little better than their Imperial counterparts. General Stillwell's much publicized personal retreat from Burma with his Chinese troops captured the public interest, but by no stretch of the imagination was this any sort of victory.

JAPANESE SUCCESS, 1941–42

Preparation and surprise were keynotes of the Japanese jungle onslaught. At the end of 1940, Col Masanobu Tsuji was tasked with running the Taiwan Army Research Station, where the logistic and tactical aspects of the planned invasion of Malaya were studied. Clothing, hygiene, disease prevention and supply were all considered, with practice manoeuvres in China in June 1941. Interestingly, the

Japanese were aware that Allied forces might be superior in strength, but with narrow routes through jungle limiting the numbers that could be effectively engaged they considered that 'the authority of the naked sword' would be conclusive. Though many orthodoxies might have to be abandoned, the terrain therefore presented 'ideal fighting conditions'. With constricted frontages, Tsuji concluded that the 250 bridges between the Japanese starting points in Thailand and northern Malaya, and their target of Singapore, were decisive tactical features. Accordingly it was decided that each infantry division should have an attached engineer regiment, and that these would practise bridge repairs in Formosa.

It would be quite wrong to claim that all Japanese troops were 'jungle trained'. Pre-1941 conscript training contained little or nothing especially relevant to tropical warfare, instead stressing such traditional skills as drill, route marches, bayonet fighting, target practice, platoon tactics and swimming. Most Japanese recruits were drawn from the open countryside or towns, while the brutal 18th Div contained many former coalminers. Few of these men would be any happier in the jungle than their adversaries; indeed, in New Guinea, when food ran out and cannibalism began, a rumour would spread amongst the Japanese that there were demons in the jungle, and some genuinely believed it. Yet most Japanese troops were experienced, as the Australian *Official History* explained:

'The tactics, equipment, and strengths and weaknesses of the Japanese army in 1941 were the products of the long war against China against stubborn soldiers lightly armed and generally ill led, but cunning guerrillas fighting on terrain which presented immense difficulties to the movement of mechanised forces. Hence largely came the Japanese skill in landing operations and road making and bridging; their changing organisation and tendency towards forming ad hoc forces; their relatively light equipment and reliance on mortars and small guns rather than on the standard field gun, and on light tanks; [and] their emphasis on envelopment tactics.'

For the many, specific jungle training was sketchy. According to Col Tsuji's account, 'The study of jungle warfare had been set down as part of the duties of the [Research Station] on Taiwan, but very little work could be done on the subject as there was no suitable jungle there. Afterwards, the advance of the Imperial Guards Division into the southern part of Indochina provided some experience, but in Indochina there was no malignant, swampy jungle as there is in Malaya.'

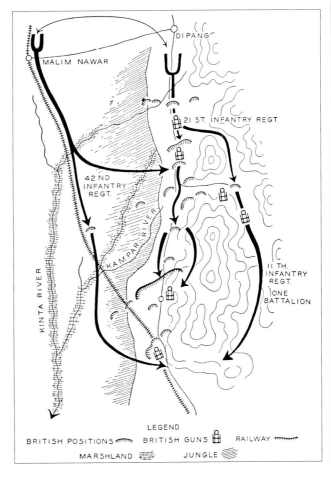

A Japanese plan showing a variation on the 'scorpion manoeuvre' as used at the battle of Kampar, Malaya, 30 December 1941–2 January 1942. The advance is in two main columns, one of which engages the 15th Indian Bde frontally, while the 42nd 'Ando' Regt follows the course of the railway through the jungle to emerge in the Allied rear.

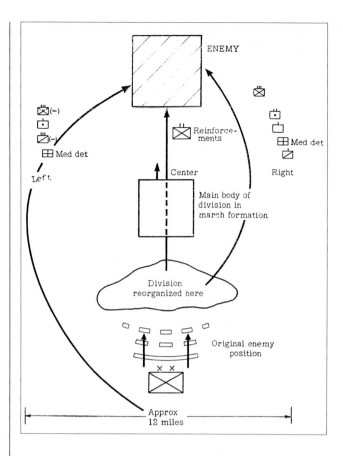

ENEMY

Reinforce-ments

Center

Right

Left

Med det

Med det

Main body of
division in
march formation

Division
reorganized here

Original enemy
position

x x

Approx
12 miles

The Japanese use of flanking
columns at infantry division level,
as depicted in the US *Handbook
on Japanese Military Forces*. The
'left' and 'right' detachments
might be several miles either
side of the main body, and might
advance a similar distance
beyond.

What knowledge had been gleaned was summarized as a minor part of the bullishly entitled pamphlet *Read Only This – And The War Can Be Won*, issued to Japanese troops en route to Malaya. Here the soldier learned to expect heat comparable to midsummer in Japan, indeed a 'world of everlasting summer' remaining warm all year round despite wet and dry seasons. Drinkable water was likely to be difficult to obtain, so troops were encouraged not only to fill their water bottles but also beer bottles or any other containers they might have at hand. How much would be needed would vary, but as a rough calculation 10 litres per man and 60 per horse was to be regarded as a minimum. This would be supplemented by coconut and pineapple juice, and liquid obtained from wisteria vines. Marches would be broken at midday to avoid the worst of the heat, and the sun protection of the issue cap supplemented by lining with grass or twigs arranged to hang over the head. Sweat running down the face in battle was best avoided by tying a bandana around the temples beneath the steel helmet. Where possible, dry clothes would be donned before going to sleep.

The 'Great Enemy' was the malarial mosquito: 'since ancient times far more have died through disease than have been killed in battle. In tropical areas, as in Japan, the majority of diseases enter through the mouth, but in South Asia you must take precautions also against mosquitoes and snakes. To fall in a hail of bullets is to meet a hero's death, but there is no glory in dying of disease… or carelessness. And a further point you would do well to consider is that native women are almost all infected with venereal disease…'. Against mosquitoes, instructions were to apply repellent, drink anti-malarial medicines and burn incense sticks. Less obviously, when a Japanese soldier encountered a dangerous snake he was advised not only to kill it, but also to swallow its liver raw and to cook its meat, this being an excellent medicine for strengthening the body.

Purely tactical advice was limited, save that however 'inferior' the British and their colonial lackeys might be, they were not to be altogether despised, since they would probably be occupying strategic points and fortifications. Therefore, 'You must not rest after crushing the enemy at the landing points, but must make a forced march, or a rapid motorised swoop, through the sweltering tropical terrain and launch an attack at once upon the main positions. In order to avoid prepared concentrations of fire, and to achieve surprise, it may frequently happen that you will traverse jungle regions or wade through swamps or paddy fields.'

Whilst 'weak-spirited Westerners' were inclined to regard jungle as impenetrable, the Japanese were to use it in order to outmanoeuvre them. In bamboo groves the best way to move was through the less dense parts, lopping off branches or making cuts so that the exposed whiteness created a route marker. When attacking into bamboo the approved method was a concerted rush from close quarters. Bamboo thickets were good to defend, but Japanese troops were warned against the 'terrible noise' of bullets crashing through, to the demoralization of the uninitiated. Movement through plantations of sugar cane could be difficult, but scouts using compasses and ladders, or climbing trees, could help maintain direction.

The supplies carried by the divisional train – weak by Western standards and mainly reliant on pack and draft animals – would be supplemented by what Japanese soldiers called 'Churchill rations', the stores abandoned by Allied troops seeking to escape encirclement. Where the enemy had the presence of mind to remove or destroy supplies, local civilians would be mercilessly robbed. In jungle terrain the emphasis would be on the resilience of the individual; as the US *Handbook of Japanese Military Forces* of October 1944 put it, 'Rapidity of the advance and vigorous attack are counted upon to overwhelm the enemy, and reliance is placed upon the ability of the Japanese soldier to live off the land, fight with the bayonet, and withstand hardship until the objective is taken. It is evident that the Japanese Army is expected to be so well trained that detailed orders are unnecessary.'

According to Col Tsuji, infantry regiments were each issued with approximately 50 trucks by the time of the invasion of Malaya, but where these were held up the advance would be continued without them – often headed by the bicycle troops. (For comparison, the establishment of a British or Indian division in 1941 included some 2,000 motor vehicles.)

What was absolutely crucial to jungle success was that existing infantry organization and tactics proved extremely well suited to the conditions. With some justice, Shelford Bidwell described the Japanese Army as 'a simple rifle and bayonet affair' – the infantry regiment and infantry division were the prime organizational units, artillery and tanks being regarded as close support weapons for the infantry. The fact that both armour and guns were less up-to-date than the Western equivalents mattered little in jungle, where space to drive, and fields of fire, were virtually non-existent. Success or failure hinged on the infantry.

* * *

The mainstay of Japanese tactical doctrine was the primacy of attack, close combat being endowed with what has been described as a 'mystic virtue'. This would doubtless have led to disaster in the open; but in jungle – and particularly by night – the Allies had no opportunity to destroy attacks at long range. In cases of doubt aggression remained effectively the default option. As the US *Handbook* would explain:

'The Japanese lay great stress on offensive actions, surprise, rapidity of movement, with all commands and staffs operating well forward in order to keep themselves constantly informed of the situation. Their tactical doctrine is based on the principle that a simple plan, carried through with power and determination, coupled with speed and manoeuvre, will so disrupt the plans of hostile forces that success will ensue. Combat orders, in both attack and defence, from the highest to the lowest unit, generally carry the admonition that the "enemy force will be annihilated". Surprise is an ever-present element, while the envelopment is the preferred form of attack. Thorough reconnaissance is also taught, and the practice of infiltration is greatly stressed. The Japanese willingness to attack a position with forces other nations would consider insufficient for the task is based on the assumption of their so called military superiority.'

This was *seishin* – a strength of will that was expected to prevail over an enemy's material and numerical superiority. In the execution of this doctrine we see not just a revival of the old spirit of the *samurai* warrior, but an assimilation of French and German tactical ideas on the attack current between 1860 and 1914. The result was a heady mixture indeed.

Offensive tactics

In the abstract, the infantry tactics in the Japanese Field Service Regulations had much in common with those of European instructions current early in World War I. The prime objectives were to locate the enemy, march towards him deploying into line, and, with or without the application of fire, close with him. If the enemy did not recoil immediately he was held by the forward elements of the attacking force, and a knockout blow was delivered by a reserve, usually around a flank or by envelopment. This basic scheme was modified slightly by the presence of light machine guns, issue of which had commenced in the 1920s. Mortars and light tanks would add strength and surprise rather than altering the essential model. The deployment from march column to assault was in four stages:

Bunshin Breaking from march column into small ones out of hostile artillery range at the beginning of the approach march.
Tenkai Deployment along the line of departure (*tenkaisen*) for an assigned combat mission.
Sokai Advance from the *tenkaisen* in small (section) columns.
Sankai Final deployment to permit firing during the last few hundred yards of the assault.

Artillery would give support according to a pre-arranged plan, the emphasis in the concluding phases being on pushing the guns close for direct assistance of the main effort, ideally to as near as 500 to 800 yards from the enemy. Reconnaissance and the driving in of enemy outposts were parts of the plan, but were seldom allowed to hold up all-out assaults. Likewise, while co-ordinated attacks were desirable they were by no means obligatory, sub-units attacking piecemeal as opportunity allowed. Maintaining unit alignment was seen as unimportant, and junior commanders would vie with each other for the honour of being allowed to make the first assault. The least suggestion of hanging back was a serious dishonour.

As unit commanders were well forward, the main tactical decision was how to balance the force prior to attack. Frequently it would be divided into two or more 'wings', the strongest of which was designated for the main effort. The attack could be made by night or day, but a common plan was to advance to the line of departure under cover of darkness before launching the assault at dawn. Ideal frontages were wincingly cramped, with a battalion having just 400 to 600 yards through which to press home with the bayonet.

Under jungle conditions these tactics were altered in that the advance would usually be in narrow parallel columns, one or more of which could move independently and wide around obstructions. This would become known to Allied officers as the 'scorpion manoeuvre', where one column gripped the defenders in its claws while the stronger tail, with its lethal sting, encircled the rear. The advance of Japanese columns into and around Allied positions, through jungle, without reference to security of flanks or to lines of supply, was initially viewed by the Allies with incredulity. Frequently the advance guard of cycle troops advanced unconcernedly down the available roads until halted by fire. Such tactics were regarded as foolhardy by European standards, but for Allied forces dependent on land lines of communication and supply there would be only two alternatives: rapid disengagement, or envelopment followed by almost certain destruction. The paucity of Japanese transport became a positive advantage under these conditions. Moreover, the Japanese achievement of sea and air superiority around and above Malaya in December 1941–January 1942 tended to blind the defence, and to open up possibilities for repeated coastal landings behind Allied front lines.

Though major frontal assaults were discouraged, many secondary attacks were launched into the teeth of the defenders, and here speed and surprise were preferred to the dubious advantage of support fire over or through the jungle. Sometimes more subtle attempts would be made to feel for 'soft spots'. One stratagem was to encourage the defender to open up with his support weapons, which would be answered by a heavy concentration of mortar fire that allowed the

Part of a well-camouflaged Japanese infantry section, including a light machine gunner, during a stream crossing; the riflemen move with fixed bayonets. Copious foliage has been used to break up the outlines of packs and helmets.

Japanese to advance unmolested. Sometimes a secondary force could achieve its objective without actually attacking, creating a noisy demonstration designed to keep the Allied force pinned and wary of moving.

Night attacks in jungle were usually executed on a narrow front with limited but well-defined objectives. Where possible they were delivered up hill – this avoided silhouetting the attackers against the skyline, and at the same time an incline helped maintain a sense of direction in darkness. Demonstrations elsewhere, perhaps accompanied by flares, would serve to distract the defenders of the objective from the direction of assault. If it was feasible, the vanguard of the night attack would advance with stealth until well within the enemy position, where they would target known heavy weapons in an attempt to silence them before the delivery of the main blow.

Ambush and deception

Ruses and deceptions were key elements. Colonel Tsuji relates that the Intendance Department supplied a thousand Thai uniforms for the invasions of Thailand and Malaya. In New Guinea, feint attacks were intended to draw the Australians out of position. Noise, or the sudden appearance of a man or two, might trick defenders into opening fire. In most jungles, and at night, English-speaking Japanese would shout instructions to retire, or for 'Corporal Smith' to step forward. Signal wires would be cut, then snipers would wait for linemen, zeroed in on the place where the break had been created. Roadblocks, booty, food, document bags and even injured troops would be booby-trapped. Few Japanese actually surrendered, but many pretended to, some of them holding a grenade in each hand. When first fired upon some Japanese would immediately fall to the ground and 'play dead'. Civilians often became caught up in deceptions, being bribed or forced to spy, give warnings, spread false information, or provide a living shield for the movement of troops. In January 1942 the British Army journal *War* described Japanese tactics thus:

'Japanese forces in Malaya are a well-trained army of gangsters, well but lightly equipped, who apply vigorous tactics combined with many ruses. Their tactics aim at rapid infiltration and outflanking of defence, and the normal method of attack has been as follows: first a number of men, dressed in shorts, open shirts and running shoes, have been sent forward to locate our positions, mixing, where possible, with the civilian population. When they have sent their information back, strong forces waiting in the rear have deployed and passed round the flanks of our positions to attack from behind.'

The most important surprise in jungle was the ambush, perhaps the commonest model featuring an anti-tank gun or machine gun placed near a bend in a road or track. Around the bend would be a block, and

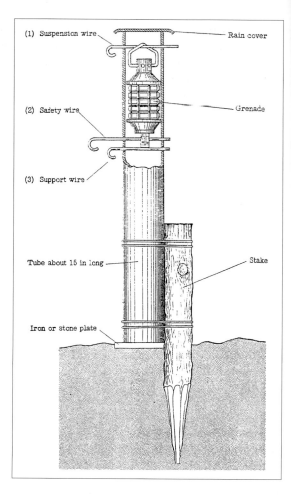

(1) Suspension wire — Rain cover

(2) Safety wire — Grenade

(3) Support wire

Tube about 15 in long —

Iron or stone plate

— Stake

One of many types of booby-trap used by the Japanese to impede jungle trails. The fuse cap of Japanese Type 91 and 97 hand grenades had to be struck on a hard surface to initiate the (imprecise) 8- or 5-second time fuse. To arm this trap the safety and support wires were withdrawn, leaving the grenade dangling inside the bamboo tube. When the suspension pin was pulled out by an Allied soldier stumbling into a trip wire, the grenade dropped on to the hard plate, igniting the fuse.

as vehicles or troops slowed the weapon would fire at point blank range. Snipers or booby-traps might add to the confusion, allowing the crew of the main weapon to keep firing or to move their equipment. Another variation was to allow Allied troops to pass an outpost before firing into their rear. A number of veterans recalled that a favourite ambush technique in jungle was to drop grenades out of trees – most devastatingly, into the back of an open-topped vehicle. A version of the tree ambush was recorded in Burma by LtCol Leonard in February 1942:

'A short way down the road we saw a British 30cwt truck, abandoned and the leading tank roared past it along the right hand ditch. Our driver considered the other side of the road better going for his wheeled carrier and drove onto the very verge beneath a tree. As we passed the tree many things seemed to happen at once; there was a harsh rattle of a light automatic. I felt as if a heavy draught horse had kicked me on the knees. I saw John Wickham and Ian slump towards each other as the carrier slithered to a stop. A moment later another burst followed the first and my left arm, by which I was bracing myself, was flung aside and I fell forward in time for my head to be missed by the third burst which, ricocheting off the back plate, filled the carrier with further splashes of lead. The Lance Naik [lance-corporal] of the carrier had been sitting on top nursing his own light machine gun and it was now that he spotted our own particular enemy perched in the tree above us, and he was not slow to demonstrate that 1/4th [Gurkhas] Lance Naiks only require one burst to achieve their object. By now the inside of the carrier was closely resembling a shambles.'

During his recovery Leonard discovered that his skin had been perforated in no less than 68 places by splinters and bullets, four of his comrades being wounded or killed. During his evacuation by ambulance he was ambushed a second time, on this occasion lying helpless in his stationary vehicle while a Japanese sniper climbed on to the roof, and another enemy soldier worked his way underneath it with an anti-tank rifle.

Machine gun tactics

While heavy weapons were of reduced importance in dense vegetation, Japanese willingness to push machine guns into the attack ensured that they remained a potent element. As the US *Handbook on Japanese Military Forces* observed:

'Machine guns normally are employed in pairs and placed well forward to support front line infantry. They go into position under cover, and advanced preparations are made so that, by opening fire accurately and with surprise effect, fire superiority may be quickly gained. Positions are selected with a view to advancing as the attack progresses. Forward movement to new positions may be by individual gun, or by pairs, depending on the type of terrain and the situation, but preference is shown for the latter. It is normal for the guns of a platoon to fire on the same target.'

The standard 7.7mm Type 92 heavy weapon – known to Allied soldiers as the 'woodpecker' from its distinctive sound – could be carried into action as a single unit mounted on its tripod, the weight being spread between three or four men by means of three poles

which slotted into bayonet-type fittings on the tripod feet. Like the older 6.5mm Type 3, this was an air-cooled Hotchkiss design. For long marches machine guns were dismounted, as described by Suzuki Murio of the 37th (Osaka) Regt:

'The guns weighed more than 50kg [110lb] each, so they were disassembled and packed on horseback for transport, but when you approached the battlefield four men put the gun back together and carried it. Two men actually manned it in action. Each man in the company was assigned a number and all the numbers one, two, three and four were assigned to the guns, while everyone else from numbers five on were in charge of the ammunition. No.2 fired the gun; because a heavy machine gun is a large weapon, No.2 could hide himself behind it. He was supposed to fire it with his hands but, bent over, he usually depressed the firing button with the top of his steel helmet… No.1 had to load the [strip], so his whole side was exposed to the enemy – No.1s got killed at a fearful rate.'

The HMGs naturally drew a good deal of fire, and, according to Suzuki, it was therefore common practice to relocate the gun after firing about 90 rounds (three feed strips). Standing up under fire was extremely hazardous, and although crews often zigzagged 'like lightning', many were shot down in the process. If crews stayed put they also risked being given away by the HMG's oiler system, which could make a visible haze during protracted fire.

The light machine guns of the infantry platoons were the bipod-mounted 6.5mm Type 11 and the more effective 7.7mm Types 96 and 99, both the latter bearing a superficial similarity to the Bren gun (all these being inspired by the Czechoslovak ZB designs). Both the Types 96 and 99 had detachable 30-round box magazines, and were mainly used as close support for the infantry squads. Having a faster rate of fire than the HMGs they could be distinguished by their sound – the Gurkha officer John Masters would describe this as an 'hysterical' chatter. Commonly, three out of the four infantry squads of a platoon were supported by an LMG, the fourth by a light mortar or grenade discharger. Technically the LMG component of the 13-man squad was four strong – a leader and three gunners. Rifles or pistols were carried by all members of the LMG team.

If anything, Japanese LMGs were intended to be handled more aggressively than Bren guns. One approved tactic was to advance with the weapon suspended from a shoulder sling firing from the hip, and both the Types 96 and 99 were fitted to take a bayonet – though how practical a lunge with a 20lb machine gun actually was, is open to question.

Machine guns of all types were the key to defensive positions, placed either singly or in groups. Commonly they did not attempt to engage at long range, but on limited sectors close in front of the position:

'Lanes of fire for these guns are cut by tunnelling through the underbrush, thus making it extremely difficult to locate them, but at the same time restricting their field of fire. Long-range machine gun fire is not practised in jungle. The guns are usually sited for cross fire. They may also be sited in ravines to deny this route of approach to the enemy, and on reverse slopes to catch troops as they come over the crest.'

One deception practised in defence was to fire only single shots when the enemy was at medium range, switching to full automatic bursts once the opposition had screwed up their courage for close assault. Retreat was alien to Japanese tactical doctrine, but in such an eventuality machine gunners were trained to stay until last, covering their comrades as they fell back. At such times they were exhorted not to think of loss, but to sacrifice themselves by firing to the last on those enemy whose advance presented the greatest danger.

ALLIED REACTION, 1942–43

British 'stay-behinds' and irregulars

The British loss of Malaya, Singapore, Hong Kong and most of Burma was a catastrophic shock, and it is commonly suggested that it led to the drastic revision of jungle warfare techniques. Yet well before Gen Percival's surrender in February 1942 it was realized that there was something seriously awry with both tactics and training. Pre-war exercises had already demonstrated that the jungle was penetrable, and belated steps had been taken during 1941.

Number 101 Special Training School was established in Singapore some months before the outbreak of war, to teach small numbers of soldiers and civilians irregular warfare and intelligence-gathering. By August 1941 the notion of 'stay-behind' parties was propounded for areas that fell under enemy domination, but this was only approved on the outbreak of war four months later. Chinese communists were now accepted as possible allies, and many would subsequently form guerrilla groups. There were minor forays behind enemy lines, and after the surrender a small number of intelligence-gatherers remained, a few of whom managed to mount sabotage and ambush actions. British and Australian 'coast watchers', as well as native scouts, continued to perform vital duties behind enemy lines in several countries.

Such activities were hampered by lack of reliable communications, the ravages of

Formation for a British platoon moving through jungle, from *Forest, Bush, and Jungle Warfare...*, August 1942. 'The platoon sergeant maintains direction through his leading section, and keeps station through the rear section.'

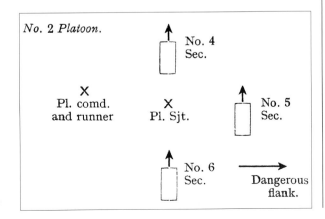

No. 2 Platoon.

No. 4 Sec.

X Pl. comd. and runner

X Pl. Sjt.

No. 5 Sec.

No. 6 Sec.

Dangerous flank.

sickness, and continual movement to avoid capture; but crucial lessons were learned about survival skills and the importance of mental attitude. As Col Spencer Chapman put it:

'My experience is that the length of life of the British private soldier accidentally left behind in the Malayan jungle was only a few months, while the average NCO, being more intelligent, might last a year or even longer. To them the jungle seemed predominantly hostile, being full of man-eating tigers, deadly fevers, venomous snakes and scorpions, natives with poisoned darts, and a host of half-imagined nameless terrors. They were unable to adapt themselves to a new way of life and a diet of rice and vegetables. In this green hell they expected to be dead within a few weeks – and as a rule they were. The other school of thought, that the jungle teems with wild animals, fowls and fish which are simply there for the taking, and that luscious tropical fruits – paw-paw, yams, breadfruit and all that – drop from the trees, is equally misleading. The truth is that the jungle... provides any amount of fresh water, and unlimited cover for friend as well as foe – an armed neutrality, if you like, but neutrality nevertheless. It is the attitude of mind that determines whether you go under or survive. There is nothing either good or bad, but thinking makes it so. The jungle itself is neutral.'

In terms of infantry tactics, the guerrilla actions taught little that was novel – indeed, the 'stay-behinds' were often months or years behind current practice and technology. For training, old manuals were amended, copied and circulated, but these were 'three years out of date' by the time they were needed; new information had to be brought in from outside by the new generation of infiltrators in Force 136.

Tactical impetus therefore came from outside, albeit from experienced officers who had served in Burma or had been perilously evacuated from Malaya. One key figure was Brig Ian Stewart, former CO of the 2nd Argylls, whose ideas were rapidly absorbed by I Australian Corps, and were taken back to the UK for incorporation into the latest training literature. Major-General Gordon Bennett, latterly commander of 8th Australian Div, also escaped to pen a series of reports on Japanese methods.

British 1942 training manuals

Although much has been made of the punningly titled Indian Army manual *The Jungle Book*, with its cartoon cover showing a hand marked 'good training' squeezing the life out of a Japanese soldier, advances in jungle tactics were incremental. Arguably the first significant step was *Forest, Bush and Jungle Warfare Against a Modern Enemy*, produced in the UK in August 1942 and reprinted in Canada within a month. The key words here were 'modern enemy'; it was now conceded that Japan was a modern, technically advanced enemy worthy of serious consideration. What was needed to face and outmatch her soldiers was a body of tactics

BATTALION DEFENSIVE POSITION - FRONTAGE DEFENCE

LEGEND

- Platoon positions and battalion H.Q. area with reserves and supporting arms.
- Mobile reserves.
----- Enemy movement.
——→ Movement of own troops.

NOTE: The action of patrols is not shown

British battalion defence, from *Forest, Bush, and Jungle Warfare Against a Modern Enemy*, published in August 1942. The deployment is as a series of platoon positions across the front, covering the jungle as well as the road. Small mobile reserves are kept to counter-attack infiltration or outflank the enemy.

that took into account lack of mobility and vision in the jungle, as well as the special problems of survival. 'Natives' were no longer viewed merely as 'second line infantry' but as the source of 'greatly superior knowledge of the country, inhabitants and language'. They were also potential guerrillas and intelligence agents; but nothing would be of any avail without properly trained and equipped infantry:

'Infantry will remain the general purpose arm. It can go anywhere and, within a dense area, it has little to fear from any arm other than enemy infantry which can outmanoeuvre it. Fighting in close country makes it desirable that infantry should be specially equipped for this purpose. Some form of hatchet (dah, machet or kukri) is essential. Four per section is sufficient, as it is seldom possible to use more than two at a time. Machine carbines [SMGs], pistols, light rifles, and knives are useful alternatives to service rifles and bayonets, which are apt to encumber men in thick forests. Because of the frequent possibility of being surprised, ability to fire weapons quickly and accurately at short ranges, as well as training to fire suddenly from the hip, is very necessary.'

Though the *dah* or short Burmese sword was sometimes used, the *kukri* was the standard sidearm of the Gurkhas, its reputation being as fearsome as its actual effect. Using it required practice, however, as Lt Donald Day of the 1/4th Gurkhas recalled:

'Gurkhas prefer the kukri to the bayonet, they can cut a man in half with it. A standard blow is a cross cut to the shoulder. They cut off heads. It is a terrifying weapon, and used in the hand of the Gurkha is lethal. I have used a kukri in anger only once. I was using it to sharpen a pencil by a haystack, and a Jap suddenly appeared around the corner, and I hit him with the kukri as I had nothing else to attack him with. My orderly was so convulsed with laughter at my ineptness, he failed to despatch the chap quickly. The Gurkhas have a strange sense of humour. I made a mess of him and my orderly finished him off.'

Edged weapons may have had great morale value, but sub-machine guns were more efficient. The heavy Thompson with its .45in ACP rounds was particularly devastating at close range, as Lt D.F.Neill of the 3/2nd Gurkhas related. He flushed several enemy from the cover of a paddy field *bund* in the Arakan, then pursued one to a dramatic denouement:

'My chest was heaving, my Tommy gun muzzle was going up and down, my eyes full of sweat. I fired three bursts and could see the rounds hitting the man's back, flicking away pieces of shirt and flesh. I had not realised the hitting power of a .45 inch bullet before. The Jap shot forward like a rag doll hit with a sledge hammer.'

While short-range arms were at a premium, *Forest, Bush and Jungle Warfare* admitted that support weapons and vehicles needed careful handling in the confines of jungle:

'Mortars, particularly the 2in mortar, are the most suitable close support weapons, and hand grenades are needed on a higher scale than normal. In the thickest

A scheme for a British infantry brigade defence, as outlined in *Forest, Bush, and Jungle Warfare...*, August 1942. It shows the company locations of the forward left-hand battalion fending off a Japanese secondary probe, while the main enemy effort hits the forward right-hand battalion with the usual two-prong enveloping attack. The lessons of six months beforehand have already been learnt: the two forward battalions hold their ground, while the reserve battalion deploys with artillery support to meet the 'scorpion's tail'.

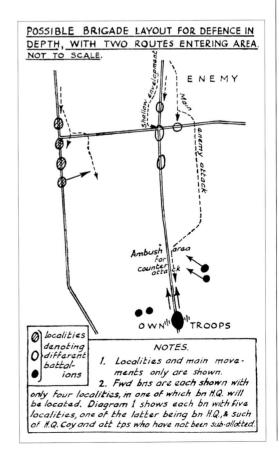

areas, surprise and guerrilla methods may have to take the place of supporting weapons. Light machine guns with tripods are useful in defence, and when the field of fire is short, fixed line fire will be found particularly useful. The use of light machine guns in the attack is limited and a reduced scale may be advisable. The Bren carrier is vulnerable in close action, particularly to small arms fire and grenades from enemy concealed in trees. Carriers require to be netted in on top for protection against grenades. They are easily concealed, and can usefully be employed in static ambushes or as mobile forts around which the infantry can base themselves. The height of the light machine gun from the ground when mounted in a carrier gives increased fire effect.'

Forest, Bush and Jungle Warfare may not have solved all tactical issues, but it correctly identified many of them. Amongst these were the problems of control; artillery observation; trail cutting, and the need for advances on wide fronts rather than in one endless column. The special morale problems of unfamiliarity, feelings of isolation, difficulty of navigation and enemy ruses were also addressed, the simplest answer being that in jungle troops would never go anywhere singly. The great significance of radio and aircraft were also recognized – though not all the ideas given on signalling were completely realistic, as for example the suggestion that the African 'tom tom' drum be used to send Morse code. Yet the most important idea promoted was that 'front lines' no longer existed:

'In considering security in overgrown country it must be constantly borne in mind that there will seldom, if ever, be a time when a definite line will separate the area under friendly control from that in the hands of the enemy. There will be no standard front with its area of 'no man's land'. It is

BELOW **An interesting diagram showing a practice close-quarter shooting range adapted for tropical conditions, with targets and firing point configured to simulate a jungle glade. (From the Indian Army manual *Close Quarter Battle*, 1945)**

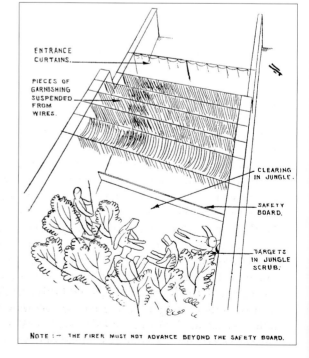

ENTRANCE CURTAINS.

PIECES OF GARNISHING SUSPENDED FROM WIRES.

CLEARING IN JUNGLE.

SAFETY BOARD.

TARGETS IN JUNGLE SCRUB.

NOTE :— THE FIRER MUST NOT ADVANCE BEYOND THE SAFETY BOARD.

Australian soldiers in close combat with Japanese troops, fighting from a foxhole under the huge buttress roots of a tree at Mount Tambu, New Guinea, in August 1943. While one man keeps the enemy pinned with short bursts from his Thompson SMG, his mate readies a No.36 grenade. In jungle conditions, especially at night, the hand grenade was a weapon of great value.

therefore necessary for every unit in the area of operations to provide itself with all round protection, whether on the move or at rest. Vegetation often crowds up to the edge of the trail, precluding observation to the flanks... All troops must be trained to act promptly, in accordance with a pre-arranged plan, to defend themselves against surprise attack.'

A key factor in gaining initiative in jungle was aggressive patrolling. Ideally all infantry were to be trained for patrols, but each battalion was now intended to have a platoon of the most competent men attached to its headquarters. These were to be selected by trials of 'a severe standard' to test the individual's endurance, initiative, knowledge of jungle lore, weapons and unarmed combat. Those who passed the tests might be given an unofficial qualification badge. For actual patrols the numbers were to be kept to a minimum, a typical 'tiger patrol' consisting of a leader and two others armed with an SMG, two rifles, a selection of grenades and a cutting tool of local pattern. Other equipment included a compass, map, water bottle, mess kit, fire kindling kit and rations. Nevertheless, 'patrols should be given a good deal of liberty in what they wear and carry. Money should be taken for buying food and information [from native villagers]. Canvas and rubber soled hockey boots (procurable in most tropical towns) are an efficient form of footwear.'

Suitable tasks for patrols up to platoon strength included ambushes; 'setting fire to the countryside, or to enemy occupied villages or administrative installations'; cutting communications; wrecking vehicles; harassing enemy encircling attacks; sniping, and the laying of mines or booby-traps on the enemy line of advance. All of this would tend to interfere with lines of communication and put the enemy 'into a state of nerves'.

While *Forest, Bush and Jungle Warfare* contained many tactical innovations, universal application would take time. This was only achieved after June 1943 with the decisions of the Infantry Committee appointed in the wake of the disastrous First Arakan campaign (September 1942–May 1943). Thereafter both Indian troops and British reinforcements would be given a two-month jungle warfare course following basic training. New literature – such as *Battle Drill for Thick Jungle*, 1943 – and new editions of *The Jungle Book* would keep trainees abreast of developments.

The Australian contribution

From July 1942 the Australians in New Guinea were confronting the problems of combat in some of the worst mountain and coastal jungle in the world. Perhaps Australia's key asset was the LHQ Training Centre (Jungle Warfare), which was established at Canungra in the Macpherson Ranges of south-east Queensland that November, with the first course graduating at Christmas 1942. For the first three weeks of the standard month-long course the men trained 12 hours a day, or all night, for six days a week. The course culminated in a six-day exercise, in which the trainees were independent of the base and living on personal rations. A special platoon commanders' course lasted six weeks.

Hard-won Australian skills would be summarized in *6th Australian Division Training Instruction No.11: Jungle Warfare*, of June 1943 – a document aimed primarily at junior leaders. Truly modern in its approach, this manual covered types of terrain, fitness, avoidance of disease, and use of tracks. It actively encouraged the use of native foods, with the rider that wherever possible the owner of the crop should be located and paid 'in coin or in kind', to avoid antagonizing the native peoples. As communication was likely to be difficult, self-reliance was vital – but this had to grow through physical fitness and the confidence born of knowledge. A crucial asset was the development of 'jungle craft' – the ability to live, move and fight in jungle, using ground and vegetation to best advantage. The soldier's ear was to become 'attuned to normal jungle noises in order that he may detect foreign or man made sounds'. His eyes must learn to notice broken twigs, trampled grass and disturbed humus betraying the passage of other troops. Points suitable for enemy ambushes were to be identified, and approached only with extreme caution. The sense of smell was not to be ignored either: it was observed that 'the Jap soldier possesses a peculiar unpleasant dank odour which is most persistent'.

The tactical synthesis contained in *6th Australian Division Training Instruction* began with an analysis of Japanese tactics, identifying specific weaknesses such as poor march discipline, careless noise and vulnerability to ambush. It was also noted that 'the individual Japanese soldier exhibits a deplorable ignorance of the common requirements of security. Many of them keep personal diaries which reveal the unit and formation to which

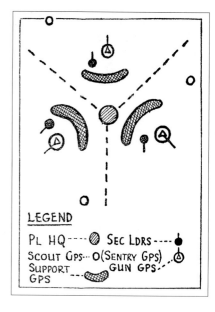

LEGEND

PL HQ ----⊘ SEC LDRS ----●
SCOUT GPS ··· O (SENTRY GPS) ·⊕
SUPPORT ─────⌒ GUN GPS·⊕
GPS

ABOVE **'Automatic defence':** a diagram showing how an Australian platoon was supposed to react on coming under attack, if it had no other orders. Each section has a scout well forward on a flank; the section leaders are in close touch with their LMG groups, and the rest of the section personnel are spread out behind in support. The diameter of the whole position was not to exceed 150 yards. (Australian 6th Division instructions, 1943)

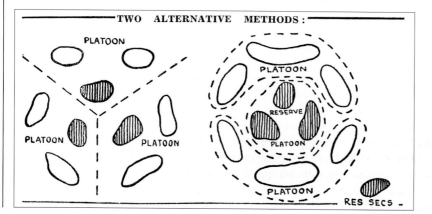

TWO ALTERNATIVE METHODS:

PLATOON

PLATOON

PLATOON

PLATOON

PLATOON

RESERVE

PLATOON

PLATOON

RES SECS

LEFT **'Automatic defence'** schemes for an Australian company. The whole position could be up to 300 yards across, allowing platoons to be up to 100 yards apart, and sections up to 50 yards. The left-hand scheme gives each platoon its own reserve section; the right-hand scheme gives the company commander a whole platoon in reserve. (Australian 6th Division instructions, 1943)

they belong, and the movements and casualties etc. of such units. They also carry marked maps and textbooks into forward areas.'

For the attack, the latest Australian doctrine recognized two forms. These were the 'encounter… carried out with all possible speed when "contact drill" fails to clear the way'; and the 'deliberate attack, planned after adequate reconnaissance', with the use of all supporting weapons. The encounter was likened to attacking in darkness or fog, but was not seen as a desperate risk: if it was executed rapidly, the enemy would also be in ignorance of the true situation. If the opposition could be panicked, or if they believed that they were victims of a major surprise, they would be likely to give way. By springing to the offensive, the attacker also maintained the initiative and kept the enemy off balance.

'Contact drills' were altered according to circumstance, mission and type of unit, but would generally be calculated to protect the axis of advance and discover the extent of the opposition by encircling manoeuvres. In the case of a reinforced company advancing through different types of jungle, the usual practice was to test the situation with an advanced patrol of platoon strength. This forward platoon would maintain contact with the main body by means of connecting files or 'getaway men'. On contact, the forward platoon would immediately attempt to deal with the opposition if it appeared weak, or to hold their axis on as wide a frontage as practicable. If the leaders were halted the second platoon would come up, moving around the right flank, or the higher flank if slopes were involved. The third platoon would move around the left or lower flank of the contact, with the result that the enemy were boxed in or at least firmly pinned. The fourth platoon, or whatever reinforcement was provided, formed the reserve for use as the company commander saw fit, ideally to move around the enemy, entirely surrounding him. In the case of deliberate attack, patrols, aerial photos and all other forms of intelligence would be used to formulate a measured plan. Wherever possible the assault would be supported on to the target, moving rapidly behind the barrage so as to prevent the defenders emerging from cover to man their weapons.

The American response

After the loss of the Philippines a whole year would elapse while America gathered strength, expanded her army, and put jungle warfare on a sustainable modern footing. The fighting on Guadalcanal in the Solomons in August 1942–February 1943 would prove a major turning point in terms of experience. New courses in jungle warfare would be established on a significant scale at Pacora, Rio Hato and Camp Pina, and the first intakes to graduate from the 60-day training would emerge in March 1943.

Perhaps surprisingly, FM 31-20 of December 1941 would remain the prime US Army jungle warfare document for almost three years, being updated by means of a relatively few pages of changes. Changes C1, issued in May 1942, stressed the role of rivers in assisting with attacks on the flanks or rear of enemy positions; the need to destroy supplies which had to be abandoned; and the necessity for forces which became isolated to keep fighting. C2, of August 1942, was primarily concerned with food hygiene, and the counter-productivity of bullying native peoples. At the end of the year C4 looked at fungal diseases and cleanliness; but it was C3, issued in September 1942, that gave general orders on suitable jungle clothing and equipment.

As before, tight-fitting clothing and wool were dismissed as unsatisfactory, as were felt and leather due to their propensity to absorb water leading to mould and rot. It was now recommended that 'Such articles should be replaced wherever possible by cotton, rubber and canvas items of clothing and equipment. As an article of outer clothing, the jungle suit, one piece, dark green, 6 to 8 ounce cotton, with zipper front extending from waistline in front, under crotch and to waistline in back, has been found highly satisfactory. Rubber soled, low canvas boots are much superior to any leather footwear. The helmet liner M1 has been found much more satisfactory than the fibre tropical helmet or the fatigue hat for jungle wear. This liner may be easily camouflaged by the use of leaves and twigs held in place by a rubber band. A head net and gloves which are mosquito proof are an inseparable part of each individual's equipment. The raincoat should be replaced by a lightweight poncho.'

The full official list of jungle clothing and equipment for the US infantryman was now specified as being:
Band, camouflage, elastic, for helmet liner M1
Boots, jungle (rubber sole, high uppers)
Socks, cushion sole
Uniform, jungle (zipper, insect proof) [i.e. one-piece suit]
Flotation bladder
Machete, 18 inch, individual
Pack, jungle (waterproof rucksack)
Bag, clothing, waterproof
Hammock, jungle
Flashlight, lightweight, jungle
Matchbox, waterproof, with compass

Survival techniques were finally comprehensively tackled by an intelligence bulletin *Living in Jungle* in September 1943.

Such was the theory: but in the first year of their war US troops suffered the same sort of shortages that plagued other armies. When the 126th Infantry reached New Guinea in September 1942 they arrived wearing uniforms which had been hastily dyed a mottled green, brown, and yellow by a Brisbane dry cleaning company. A few months later Gen Byers struggled forward to meet his men on the same front, determined to offer them some reward or comfort for their bravery. He was greeted with voluble demands for 'pants' for the many dysentery cases who were now fighting half naked. The one-piece jungle suit was in fact found less than perfect in practice, and improvements were soon being sought. On Guadalcanal, William Manchester recalled the Marines looking 'more like tramps than soldiers', wearing 'stinking dungarees', with helmets rusted red, surviving on mouldy rations and quinine.

How much there was to learn would be apparent on New Georgia as late as 1943. Here the US Army would come up against Japanese night infiltration tactics and 'jitter parties' for whom training as yet had no

US forces landing supplies on and evacuating wounded from Guadalcanal, Solomon Islands, during the six-month campaign in 1942–43; at many places the forest grew right down to the water's edge. At this date both Army and Marines wore uncovered helmets and fatigue clothing in shades of olive drab; to judge from their appearance, these men have been in the jungle for several weeks. Note the heap of stretchers (litters) in the foreground. Victory on Guadalcanal was hard-won, with 6,000 US battle casualties and another 9,000 sick; but it proved that US Marine and Army infantry could meet and master the Japanese, even before America built up her eventually massive naval and air superiority in the Pacific. The Japanese lost more than twice as many troops; but they still managed to evacuate some 13,000 men in early February 1943, fighting a skilful delaying campaign while they retreated. (US National Archives)

answer. The 169th Infantry bore the brunt, as recorded by the official historian: 'The imaginations of the tired and inexperienced American soldiers began to work. The phosphorescence of rotting logs became Japanese signals. The smell of the jungle became poison gas. Men of the 169th told each other that Japanese nocturnal raiders wore long black robes and came with hooks and ropes to drag Americans from their foxholes.'

In the aftermath of battle it was discovered that many of the casualties sustained were caused by friendly fire. Attempting to advance through thick defended jungle, using traditional tactics, and continually harassed by air raids, the entire 43rd Div came close to a collective nervous breakdown; upwards of 2,000 men were recorded as psychiatric cases.

Infantry and tanks

As early as 1942 Allied armour obtained a clear lead over the Japanese, whose tanks were outdated and vulnerable, and were anyway seldom encountered in any strength. In the confines of jungle the vital problems were getting tanks to where they were needed, and tactical co-operation with infantry. As in built-up areas, tanks were vulnerable to ambush if not closely supported. Information was readily shared between Britain and the US, and current British thinking was summed up for American tankers in the *US Intelligence Bulletin* of September 1943.

In the approach march it was considered best that most of the tank strength should move in a close, compact group some distance back from the leading infantry. In jungle no more than one platoon, of four tanks, was to be incorporated with the head of the column, and even here they were not actually to lead, since they were 'too easily held up by demolitions and obstacles'. In thick jungle attacking presented particular problems, since it was unlikely that tanks would be able to leave the roads or trails:

'Therefore not more than one platoon will be used in the attack itself, although more should be available and ready to exploit success. The actual method of attack is governed by the amount of fire support available. If it is considered sufficient to neutralise enemy antitank fire, tanks can slightly precede the bulk of the infantry, which, however, should follow closely. Where less fire support is available, the arrival of tanks on the objective should be timed to coincide with that of the infantry. In either case some infantry should advance on either flank level with the leading tanks to prevent enemy tank hunting parties – which may have survived the artillery barrage – from attacking the tanks with grenades or similar weapons. In addition to the barrage and close support of infantry, it will often be necessary for tanks to cover their advance with smoke from their own projectors, or, if these are not fitted, from mortars.'

Such an attack obviously required careful timing, and was to be 'practiced as a drill by all infantry', but was well worthwhile as the tanks were of 'great morale value'. Australian tacticians likewise observed that armour should never outstrip the infantry, whose duty it was to cover them against ambush or 'swarming attacks'.

In open spaces within jungle country the main role of the tank was to deal with hostile armour, if any, though the heavier types were also suitable for attacking enemy positions in the open. Where infantry lacked their own transport they could ride forward on the tanks; they could co-operate in the clearing of woods and gullies, with the tanks pushing around the flanks and rear of obstacles so that they could deal with any enemy driven into the open. Tanks were never to be sent into villages unless preceded by infantry. In defence and withdrawal, armour was admitted to be of marginal value unless deployed with a striking or counter-attacking force, although in an emergency they could be used to 'ferry out the rearmost parties of infantry'.

Dealing with bunkers in combined infantry and tank assaults was a skill that the British learned painfully in the Arakan, thereafter becoming something of an art form. Once enemy positions were located, both arms held back while the tanks pounded the position with high explosive. This not only stunned the opposition but blew away foliage and camouflage. Delay-fused high explosive rounds could then be fired into suspicious mounds, thus collapsing the larger bunkers. Finally, as the infantry assault went in, the tanks switched to armour piercing ammunition, which could be aimed directly into weapon slits from close range. As these solid shot did not explode they could be fired fairly close to friendly troops, who would toss grenades into foxholes and doorways before winkling out any remaining resistance with sub-machine gun and bayonet.

Such tactics would prove highly effective, inflicting large numbers of enemy casualties; but tanks did not have everything their own way. Jungle impeded observation to such a degree that tank commanders were often compelled to keep their turret hatch open; it was not unknown for them to engage with pistols and grenades as well as machine guns, and quite a few were sniped as they did so. Corporal

US Marines in the SW Pacific, winter 1943 or spring 1944. They wear the USMC two-piece reversible camouflage-printed 'uniform, utility, HBT, camouflage, P1942', first issued to Raiders and snipers in mid-1943 (see Plate A2). On the heavily forested islands of Bougainville and New Britain the three-colour printed scheme was practical; against the paler background and more open terrain of coral atolls in the Gilbert, Marshall and Caroline Islands it was found too conspicuous, and was discarded in favour of plain green utilities. The camouflaged helmet cover was retained, mostly as a proud sign of the Corps – in the same way that Australian troops clung to the 'Digger' hat despite its practical drawbacks in jungle. (US Marine Corps)

A Stuart M3 Light tank of B Sqn, 7th Light Cavalry, Indian Army, on operations on the Imphal plain, Burma, in March 1944. Tanks such as the Stuart and the Lee M3 Medium were considered adequate for the Far Eastern theatre long after their replacement as battle tanks in the West; they very seldom clashed with the inferior Japanese armour, and were an invaluable support for infantry. They needed infantry support in their turn, however, given the enemy's reliance on short-range infantry AT weapons; here a mesh of iron rods and heavy wire has been fixed over the Stuart's glacis plate as a defence against Japanese hand-placed mines. (H.Travis)

Arthur Freer, a radio operator with the 3rd Carabiniers, recorded an alarming incident near Imphal when his own commander collapsed back inside the turret; the remaining crew slammed the lid and fired all weapons in the direction of an enemy bunker before driving over it. They administered morphine to their commander, but:

'The squadron leader was hit by a bullet under the chin and it came out of the top of his steel helmet. Under his body we found a grenade, which he had been about to throw, without a handle [safety lever – it should therefore have detonated] and we had it in the tank with us amongst all that ammo, 120 rounds HE, and couldn't understand why it hadn't exploded. Paddy Ryan started to unscrew the base plate to look inside. I told him to get outside the tank while he did it. So he walked off into the paddy, took the base plate off, the cap had been struck, and the fuse burnt all the way round to the detonator and burnt out. Fortunately for us it was a dud fuse.'

US Army advice on tank/infantry co-operation, as given in FM 72-20 *Jungle Warfare* of October 1944, was almost identical to the British doctrine, stressing the need for tanks engaged in smashing enemy positions to be 'surrounded by infantry patrols which reconnoitre for routes of advance, anti tank guns, tank traps, or other anti tank obstacles, and protect the tank from tank hunting parties'. Communication between the armour and infantry was vital, either by radio or by telephone link between the infantry leader advancing immediately behind a tank and the tank leader inside the tank.

(continued on page 41)

IMPROVEMENTS IN JUNGLE UNIFORMS & EQUIPMENT
1: L/Cpl, Vickers MMG No.1, 1st Bn Manchester Regt; Singapore, October 1941
2: US Marine, 2nd Marine Raider Bn; Bougainville, November 1943
3: AB, Royal Australian Navy Commandos; Queensland, September 1944

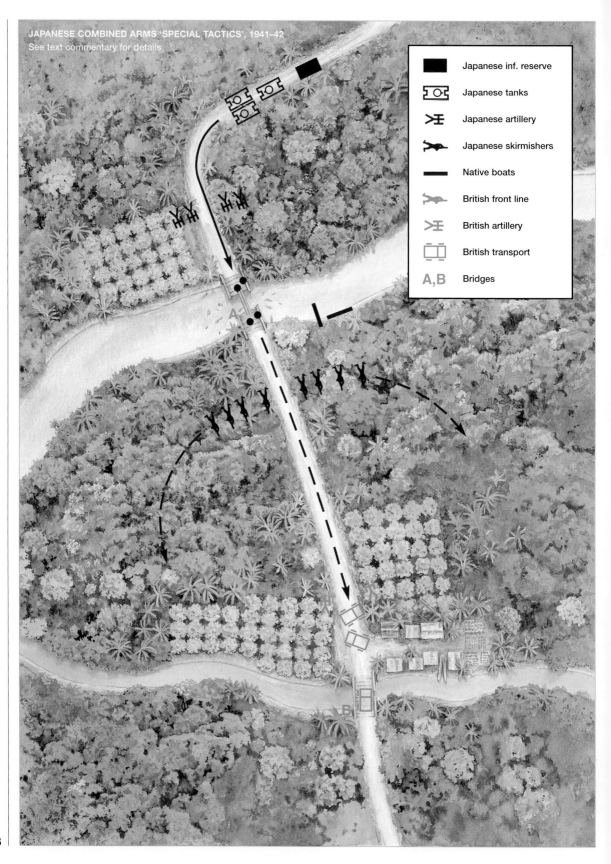

JAPANESE COMBINED ARMS 'SPECIAL TACTICS', 1941–42
See text commentary for details

■	Japanese inf. reserve
	Japanese tanks
	Japanese artillery
	Japanese skirmishers
▬	Native boats
	British front line
	British artillery
	British transport
A,B	Bridges

B

JAPANESE NIGHT ATTACK, 1943
See text commentary for details

Rifleman

Section leader

1

2

3

4: Japanese infantryman equipped for night attack

C

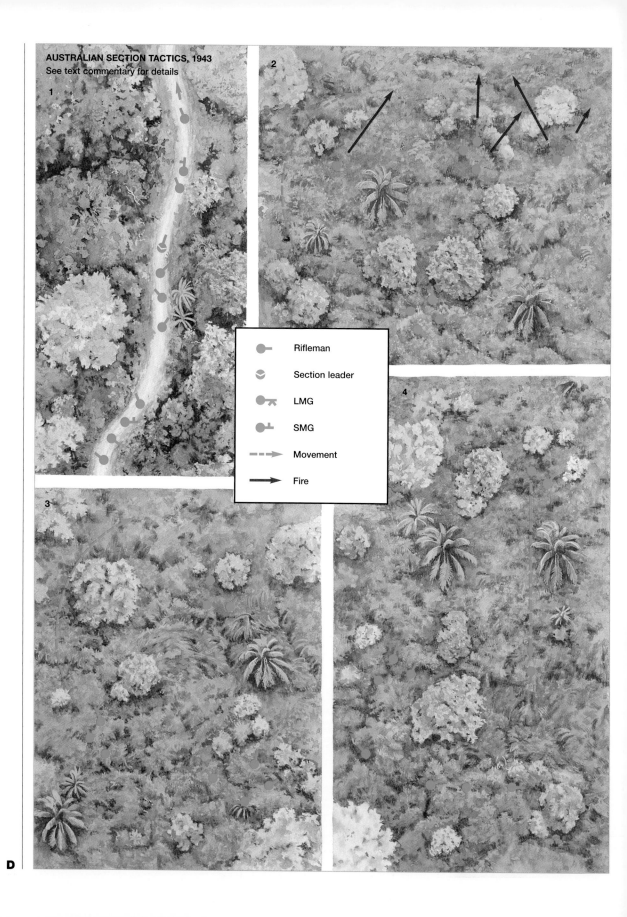

AUSTRALIAN SECTION TACTICS, 1943
See text commentary for details

1

2

3

4

Rifleman

Section leader

LMG

SMG

- - - ➤ Movement

——➤ Fire

D

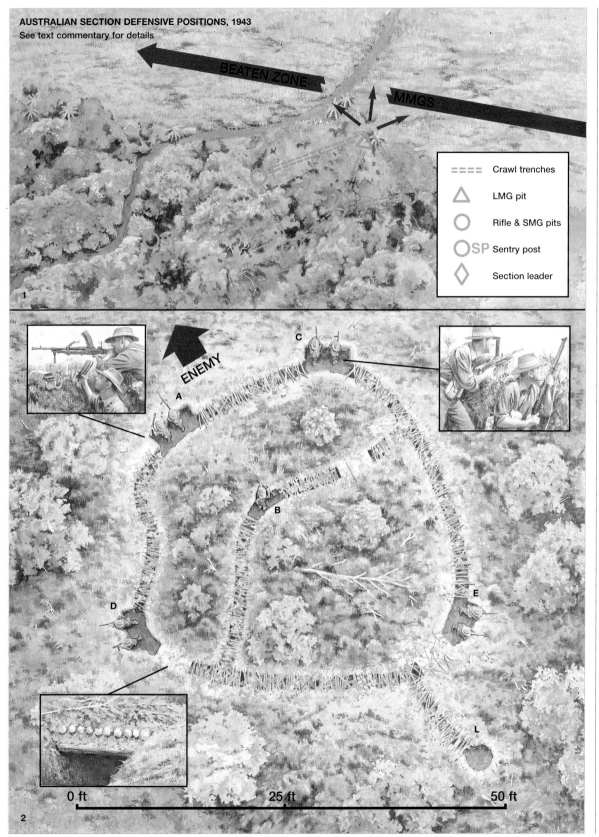

AUSTRALIAN SECTION DEFENSIVE POSITIONS, 1943
See text commentary for details

BEATEN ZONE

MMGS

Crawl trenches

LMG pit

Rifle & SMG pits

SP Sentry post

Section leader

1

ENEMY

A

C

B

D

E

L

0 ft   25 ft   50 ft

2

E

US ARMY PATROL, BOUGAINVILLE, 1944
See text commentary for details

F

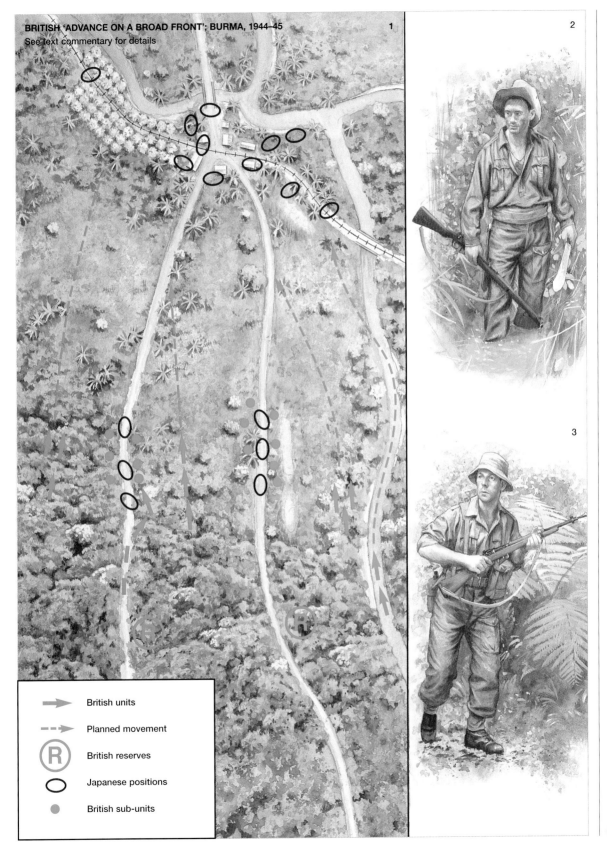

BRITISH 'ADVANCE ON A BROAD FRONT'; BURMA, 1944–45

See text commentary for details

1

2

3

→ British units

⇢ Planned movement

Ⓡ British reserves

◯ Japanese positions

● British sub-units

G

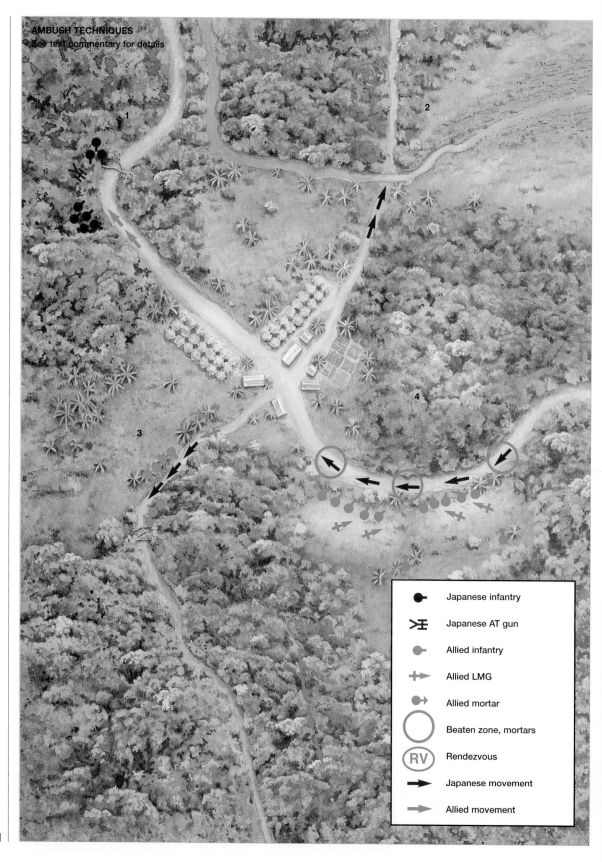

AMBUSH TECHNIQUES
See text commentary for details

●	Japanese infantry
⋇	Japanese AT gun
●	Allied infantry
╺╋►	Allied LMG
●►	Allied mortar
◯	Beaten zone, mortars
RV	Rendezvous
➤	Japanese movement
➤	Allied movement

H

US Marine tactics of 1944 linked the familiar tank/infantry combination with flame-thrower and demolition teams following in their wake. Any opposition not dealt with by the leading units would be bypassed, but before the defenders could recover and open fire on the flanks and rear of the passing tanks the bunkers would be burned and blown by the demolition squads. On Saipan each Marine regiment would be allotted 18 Shermans, four flame-thrower tanks and two light tanks. Similar methods were later used on Okinawa, but there the distance between tanks and infantry was varied to take account of the type of opposition encountered and the amount of ground cover, with the armour ranging anything up to 800 yards ahead of the infantry. Ideally artillery, tanks and infantry would all be integrated, and one method of achieving this was to carry a forward observer for the artillery in one of the tanks. In the event of loss of friendly infantry cover the artillery observer could then call down air-burst fire over his own position.

LONG RANGE PENETRATION, 1943–44

Orde Wingate and the Chindits

One of the most controversial episodes in the history of jungle warfare was the advent of Long Range Penetration, or LRP, as the essential tactic of the British 'Chindit' forces in 1943. Like his new methods, MajGen Orde Wingate attracted both adulation and vitriolic criticism. Messianic in character, and by turns brilliant, suicidal, inspirational and downright eccentric, Wingate was not an obvious choice for leadership, nor indeed for the special stresses of the jungle. According to Gen Bill Slim he was 'a strange, excitable, moody creature'; for Gen Pownall he was a genius, but 'quite a bit mad'.

Three things conspired to make Wingate the man of the hour. The first was his experience in organizing Special Night Squads of Jewish volunteers against Arab terrorists in Palestine from 1936 to 1939, and in commanding Gideon Force during the 1941 invasion of Ethiopia. Wingate's second advantage was his total commitment and determination – what Slim would call 'a fire to ignite other men'. His third asset, and that which least endeared him to his contemporaries, was that – like David Stirling, founder of the SAS – Wingate was identified by those in authority as a man of action whose exploits might catch the attention of the press, thereby turning defeat into public relations success. His methods offered the opportunity to take the fight to the enemy, and by beating them, even on a limited scale, he would demonstrate that they were no 'jungle supermen'. Perhaps worst of all from the point of view of Wingate's colleagues and immediate superiors, he had the ear of Winston Churchill, and was not afraid to name-drop.

Wingate first reached Delhi in March 1942, and was soon reconnoitring Burma in the company of Maj Mike Calvert – the officer in charge of the Bush Warfare School – with a view to promoting guerrilla operations against the Japanese. What Wingate devised was genuinely revolutionary, and became a model for many jungle warfare operations long after 1945. The Japanese successes had been based on penetration and infiltration, and Wingate proposed to answer this with 'counter-penetration'. As he summarized it in *General Rules for the*

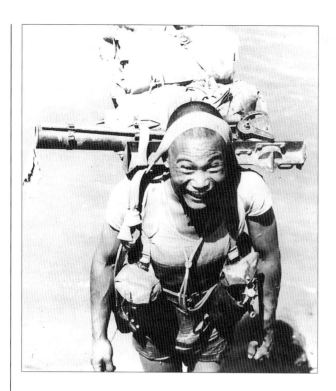

A rifleman of 4/6th Gurkhas during a river crossing in Burma. His heavy load – carried in traditional fashion with a head strap or 'tump line' – includes a 2in mortar. The Gurkhas were the only type of Indian Army unit accepted by Gen Wingate for his Chindit columns. Although they were recruited high in the Himalayan foothills, far above any region of tropical forest, their legendary adaptability and endurance proved perfectly equal to the challenge of jungle warfare.

Forces of Deep Penetration, his plan envisaged 'the operation of regular columns of high calibre in the heart of the enemy's war machine, engaging targets he is unable adequately to protect, and thus compelling him to alter his plans, thus causing a situation of which our main forces are able to take advantages'. In time, Wingate's 77th Indian Inf Bde were named 'Chindits', from the (mispronounced) name of the mythical beasts whose statues guard the entrances of Burmese temples.

The Chindit columns would each be about 400 strong, the main fighting strength being a company of infantry, plus a 'commando' platoon, a reconnaissance platoon and a heavy weapons platoon. The Royal Engineers of the commando platoon were to provide demolitions and booby-traps. The reconnaissance troops were led by a British officer of the Burma Rifles, but the other ranks would be recruited from Kachin and Karen tribesmen. The heavy weapons carried were limited to two Vickers machine guns and two 3in mortars: the marching infantryman with his rifle, sub-machine gun or Bren was to be the mainstay of action. The essential transport was provided by mules, specially silenced by having their vocal cords doctored before the mission.

Where 'low' jungle had to be forced Wingate was a hard taskmaster, using a system where a whole platoon at a time would form a 'cutting party' in arrowhead formation. Two or three men at the point would cut the usual narrow path, while more behind them on either flank would broaden the passage. More men and animals could pass more quickly, but the effort required was merciless. Resupply would be by air, freeing the Chindits from roads and vehicles. Virtually all Chindit battles would be essays in minor infantry tactics.

Contrary to popular perception, the Chindit did not start as a highly trained member of 'special forces', the companies in fact being drawn from a number of existing British and Indian regiments. The 13th Bn King's Liverpools, for example, were arguably very far from an elite, being composed of men with an average age of 33, sent to India for internal security duties. During preparatory training about a quarter of the battalion were weeded out as unsuitable for the ordeal ahead, these 'Jossers' being replaced by men from reinforcement centres and other units. Those who made the grade became known as the 'Pukka King's'.

Initially about half the Chindits were Gurkhas, and Wingate would accept no other Indian troops. According to Maj Bernard Fergusson of the Black Watch, it was no real handicap that the majority of the British Chindits were townsmen from Liverpool, Manchester and Birmingham, since acclimatization to the jungle could be achieved within months; countrymen possessed little advantage, since jungle was equally alien to them. Nevertheless, training exercises at Saugor and Jhansi quickly exposed shortcomings in some of the proposed Chindit equipment, as Fergusson recorded:

'Two unexpected horrors were added to the march. First, a new type of pack was issued called the Everest pack. This is by no means a bad gadget, but one has to have plenty of careful fitting before using it, or the weight is thrown on to the ball of the foot, with dire results for your feet. Secondly we were all issued with new boots, of an inferior pattern; and after a week's marching the casualties were innumerable. My recollections of the march are few and dim, but quite horrible…'

As supplementary to conventional forces, the Chindit column was intended for hit-and-run actions, and its mobility was to enable it to move away from better armed opponents, or larger numbers, into areas where 'the enemy will be unable or afraid to follow'. In extreme emergency the columns were taught to disperse into small parties for later rendezvous.

The other side of the coin was that without a constant link to civilization, Chindit casualties had a relatively poor prognosis: some had to be left behind, and a few received overdoses of morphine when all

Chindits carry a wounded comrade along a jungle trail. During Operation 'Longcloth' in February–April 1943 the most serious casualties often had to be left behind, sometimes with a merciful overdose of morphine but usually simply with water and their weapon, to take their wretched chances with the jungle and the Japanese. In all, the 3,000-strong force lost some 800 men, and only about 600 of the survivors were ever again passed fit for active service. During Operation 'Thursday' the following February, air evacuation was a practical option; but the unexpectedly long time the force was kept in action, in a conventional infantry role for which they were not equipped, again caused very heavy casualties. The subsequent medical examination of one brigade which had gone in 2,200 strong found that just 118 of all ranks were fit for active service. (QLR)

British officers of a Chindit column, Operation 'Thursday', February 1944; at left is Maj Michael Calvert, an early exponent of jungle warfare techniques and the most successful column commander in 1943, who became a legendary figure in British special forces. Comparing the appearance of these soldiers with those illustrated on page 7 underlines just how far British front line practice had come in little more than two years. At right, an officer holds one of the M1 .30cal carbines, first seen by Capt Richard Rhodes James as part of a Chindit air drop: 'We unpacked them from their crates and appraised them, light and rather flimsy weapons but delightfully handy. We retired to a corner of the jungle and practised with them. They were apt to jam on the first few rounds but soon cleared and were refreshingly free from recoil. They looked as if they would be difficult to clean in the rains...' (IWM MH7287)

else was hopeless. As with casualties, so with malcontents: without the means for confinement, and with loss of pay meaningless, discipline in Chindit forces had to become largely a matter of self-control. Theoretically flogging had been abolished in 1881, but Wingate would have at least two of his men lashed when all other options failed.

Food was a vexed question, since a balance had to be struck between overloading and slow starvation. For want of anything better K-rations were often carried, but these were not designed for long-term use and were deficient in nutrients. Among their least appealing contents were packets of Dextrose tablets – so revolting 'even the mules refused them'. One of the main staples of the Chindit diet was the hard *shakapura* biscuit, hard tack that could be ground down into a kind of porridge; this was roundly praised by Wingate for its promotion of healthy bowel movement. Nuts, cheese and raisins provided protein and sugar, but played havoc with imperfect teeth or dentures. The Gurkhas got rice, which was habitually carried in a spare sock, and originally cooked in large pots; Wingate insisted that preparation be speeded by the use of smaller vessels in which the water boiled more quickly. Another curious discovery of Chindit cookery was the value, and the danger, of bamboo: whilst it made good smokeless kindling when shaved finely, it had to be split before use – unsplit bamboo thrown on a fire burst with a report like a rifle shot, and the splinters could injure the unwary. Water bottles were supplemented by Arab-style *chaguls* or bags, which kept their contents cool by soaking and evaporation.

If columns separated, logistics deteriorated, since locating very small bodies of men and supplying them by air was well nigh impossible. Wingate issued an orange scarf with a map of Burma printed on it, which could be worn on the head as a recognition aid in lieu of the usual bush hat. The beard became another Chindit trademark, but had practical value: the absence of 400 shaving kits meant lighter baggage, and the beard served both as instant face camouflage and as a first line of defence against mosquito and tick. At times Wingate positively ordered his men not to shave, but this was relaxed from time to time. Another of Wingate's foibles was opposition to smoking, and ideally he would have banished cigarettes from the Chindit rations, due not only to the 'continuous coughing and expectorating they cause', but their addictiveness and promotion of irritability.

Operation 'Longcloth'

This first Chindit operation was not a success, costing the attackers more men and resources than the Japanese. This was at least in part because it had originally been planned as just one part of a multi-pronged offensive, to include advances in the Arakan and Stillwell's push into Burma at the head of a Chinese force, but in the event it was an isolated affair. Several of Wingate's columns were rapidly located by the enemy, and the mission degenerated into messy skirmishes many of which collapsed into exercises in escape and evasion. Columns of exhausted, famished men battled to extricate themselves from the enemy and the jungle, and Brigade HQ ended up as five small parties. The 'Pukka King's' were badly hit, returning to India with just 384 men of their original complement of 721. Major Fergusson's column ran into the enemy at Bonchaung, with bloody results. Fergusson himself heard the story from one of his wounded men:

'They had walked head on into a lorry load of Japanese standing in the village; he thought they had just climbed into it after cross-examining the villagers. They had killed several of them immediately... They thought they had killed everybody, for the loss of two killed and Bill Edge and one or two others wounded... John was waiting only to collect his platoon, when suddenly a new machine gun had opened up, and hit him and several more. While he was telling me this, there was a sudden report just beside my ear, and I spun round to find Peter Dorans with a smoking rifle, and one of the "dead" Japs in the road writhing.'

A forward command post of 2nd Bn East Lancashire Regt in the 'Railway Corridor' of Burma, 1944. Note the radio operator, left, and the Tommy-gunner, second right, for close defence – apparently with two taped-together magazines fitted to his weapon. (QLR)

The most successful column was Maj Calvert's. Railway traffic was comprehensively sabotaged, two large bridges near Nankan blown up and the line cut in many places. When the enemy tried to regain the initiative Calvert was ready with covering parties and ambushes: 'At one stage a group of the enemy really got the jitters and decided to chance their all in a charge. They came at us yelling their heads off but for some reason we shall never know they chose a spot which meant crossing open country with no cover. Every one of them died.' With pursuit discouraged, Calvert led his men to safety, recrossing the River Chindwin.

Operation 'Thursday'

Following the first operation, detractors would have liked to abandon Long Range Penetration, but the Chindits had value far beyond the material. As Wingate explained to a journalist, 'Most of my Chindits are not in their first youth, but between 28 and 35… If ordinary family men from Liverpool and Manchester can be trained for specialised jungle war behind enemy lines, then any fit man in the British Army can be trained to do the same, and we show ourselves to the world as fighting men second to none, which I believe we are.'

Despite the brave words, Chindit tactics were radically redefined in the light of experience. For the Operation 'Thursday' expedition of 1944 a still greater emphasis would be placed on air supply and co-operation, courtesy of the USAAF Col Philip Cochran and his No.1 Air Commando. Two-thirds of the much expanded Chindit force would actually be inserted behind enemy lines from the air, both by glider and conventional aircraft. Bulldozers landed in the early stages would be used to clear jungle landing strips for larger aircraft such as the C-47 Dakota. Once on the ground the Chindits would still seek to disrupt supply routes and ambush the enemy, but would operate from 'strongholds'.

Using a big-game hunting metaphor, Wingate regarded a stronghold overlooking a landing or dropping zone as a *machan* or shooting platform, towards which the Japanese 'tiger' might be tempted. Strongholds would threaten the enemy, but at the same time be inaccessible by road and, ideally, surrounded by hills. The enemy would be denied the use of heavy equipment, while columns of the Special Force could orbit the position to take him by surprise. From the airstrips of the strongholds the wounded and sick could be flown out, rather than being abandoned as had previously been necessary. The strongholds themselves would have permanent garrisons, with light artillery flown in to bolster the defence. Amazingly, Wingate also saw the stronghold as a sort of demesne with shops and other facilities, into which entertainments such as the divisional dance band could ultimately be airlifted. The parallel with US tactics in Vietnam a quarter of a century later is inescapable: but the stronghold was quintessentially British. At 'Blackpool', for example, the

The Chindit defence around the 'Blackpool' stronghold (originally codenamed 'Clydeside') during Operation 'Thursday', 1944, from an official report prepared by Maj John Masters. The cricketing terms used to identify the individual positions must have been impenetrable to all but the best informed of English-speaking Japanese intelligence officers. Masters, who later became a best-selling novelist, left a striking account of his part in Operation 'Thursday' in his war autobiography *The Road Past Mandalay*.

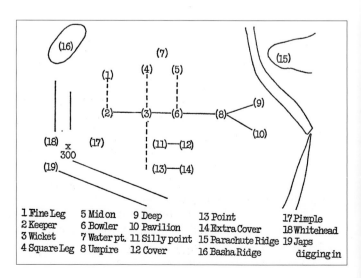

1 Fine Leg	5 Mid on	9 Deep	13 Point	17 Pimple
2 Keeper	6 Bowler	10 Pavilion	14 Extra Cover	18 Whitehead
3 Wicket	7 Water pt.	11 Silly point	15 Parachute Ridge	19 Japs
4 Square Leg	8 Umpire	12 Cover	16 Basha Ridge	digging in

Men of the 2nd East Lancashires help load a USAAF transport for the supply of forward elements in the jungle, northern Burma, 1944. A sizeable transport fleet was a major advantage for the British Empire forces; it was an asset that the Japanese had always neglected, and by this stage of the war the Allies enjoyed air superiority over SE Asia. The simultaneous demands of the Kohima and Imphal battles greatly reduced the priority that could be given to air resupply of the second Chindit operation, and was one of the factors that led to the force being absorbed into overall Allied operations and losing its special mission. (QLR)

defensive posts were named after the fielding positions on a cricket pitch – with 'point' and 'extra cover' being positioned between the Japanese line of approach and the 'wicket'.

Another key tactical deployment would be the 'block'. These were seen as temporary positions astride the enemy lines of communication, being maintained only so long as was practicable, to prevent enemy resupply and draw in forces to be ambushed. By their very nature blocks were accessible to roads, and would be abandoned as soon as the enemy brought up superior force.

With fresh experience of the importance of close-range weaponry in jungle, Brig Derek Tulloch was sent to London to evaluate and where possible obtain the latest equipment. A number of silenced pistols were gathered from the Special Operations Executive and, more importantly, new Sten guns and portable 'Lifebuoy' flame-throwers were added to the Chindit arsenal. Despite the rarity of Japanese armour in deep jungle, PIAT anti-tank weapons were used, both for blasting enemy positions and engaging trucks, which 'just disintegrated' with a direct hit. American .30cal M1 carbines were also acquired for the first time.

Though resupply was better in 1944 than it had been the previous year, individual Chindits still carried considerable burdens. One account speaks of standard 37 Pattern small packs being modified by the addition of a 37 Ptn ammo pouch sewn to each side. In the 7th Bn, Nigeria Regt, LtCol C.P.Vaughan noted that in addition to a personal weapon and ammunition, two grenades and a Bren magazine, his African soldiers' normal load included a complete change of clothes, four pairs of socks, mess tin, mug and eating utensils, water bottle and *chagul*, water sterilizing kit, field dressing, washing kit, anti-malarial tablets, groundsheet, anti-gas cape, rope, entrenching tool, machete, clasp knife and five days' rations. Though officers could delete one or two items, most also carried a watch, compass, torch, maps and pencils, and even a lightweight jungle hammock. Some authorities speak of 40lb loads, but this is certainly an underestimate.

With Operation 'Thursday' the initiative shifted decisively away from the Japanese, but the jungle infantry battle remained close and personal, particularly when night actions were attempted. Captain Richard Rhodes James recalled:

'The King's Own set out on the following evening to operate in roughly the same area as the Gurkhas. Again we waited for them and again the news... was bad. During the night a large gap had appeared in one of the columns, the breaking of one of our golden rules. Unfortunately the gap appeared between the fighting group and what was known rather anatomically as the 'soft belly'. The Japs, who were lying up off the track, were quick to spot this and engaged the soft belly which was now almost half a mile behind the head of the column. There was confusion, and a Jap officer rushing down the track severed the head of a King's Own officer; the Jap was killed immediately afterwards by a burst of Sten. Somehow out of all this confusion the King's Own managed not only to extricate themselves but also to inflict more casualties than they received...'

It has been claimed – oddly – that Gen Slim's decision to absorb the Chindit force under the command of higher formations for conventional operations after Wingate's premature death in an air crash on 24 March was motivated by personal jealousy; the general's own statement was that by August 1944 the Chindits 'had shot their bolt'. The Special Force was actually disbanded in India only in early 1945, but by August 1944 many of its units had been fought to a standstill in punishing conventional infantry battles. A more interesting explanation for the decision was provided by Adml Mountbatten, Allied Supreme Commander South-East Asia: there was no more need for Chindits, because 'we are all Chindits now'.

FM 72-20: US TACTICS, 1944

The definitive US Army text on the subject was Field Manual 72-20 *Jungle Warfare*, which finally appeared in October 1944. As with the British, US theory gained from the work of raiding forces, perhaps most importantly the 5307th Composite Unit, later known as 'Merrill's Marauders', whose 400-man teams fought in Burma in February–August 1944 – the only US ground combat unit in that theatre.

The new manual acknowledged that the infantryman 'fights two enemies – man and nature'; but fighting the jungle itself was pointless, since the individual had to adapt to conditions. Half of FM 72-20 was therefore devoted to health, hygiene, acclimatization, and plants and animals. The general rule with the latter was, don't bother them and they won't bother you, the main exceptions being the ubiquitous mosquito and the various other insects which transmitted disease. Fortunately, medical advances had kept pace with tactical, and by now quinine was being supplanted by new drugs, atabrine and mepacrine; the rate of infection fell rapidly. Many of the Pacific Islands were free of snakes, but any encountered were best treated in the same way 'as a high explosive "dud"', and left alone. In the event of a bite the snake was to be killed and shown to medical personnel, so that the correct treatment could be administered; even so, tourniquets and the sucking out of poison were recommended.

Weapons and clothing

It was now stated that there was no such thing as 'impenetrable jungle... no terrain is impassable to troops who have been trained to make their way over it'. Attitudes to weaponry had come a long way since 1941; it was now seen as axiomatic that, though difficult to transport, hand grenades and mortars were 'highly effective jungle weapons; small calibre weapons and ammunition, though less difficult to transport, are inadequate by themselves for the accomplishment of any large scale mission'. Grenades were particularly recommended as invaluable against dug-in positions; ideally, each rifleman was to carry five or six. Other personal arms would include the rifle, carbine, pistol, SMG and trench knife. The short bayonet was preferred over the long, as it was less likely to become entangled in vines and foliage. Memoirs relate the introduction of pump-action shotguns, 60mm mortars adapted for hair-raising 'direct fire', and the issue of M1919A6 .30cal LMGs with bipods and shoulder stocks.

Advice on clothing had not altered much, but the 'combat suit, two piece, herringbone twill' was now recommended as 'highly satisfactory'. Care of clothing and equipment received detailed attention, with advice on hanging clothing and equipment off the ground during the night, the protection of weapon breeches with oil-soaked rags, and how to cope with the humidity which swelled the wooden stocks of weapons.

Defensive tactics

Defences were not linear, but arranged as a series of mutually supporting 'defensive islands'. Where lack of fields of fire precluded support fire, the shoulder-to-shoulder protection of a perimeter of positions – difficult to infiltrate – was the next best proposition. Outposts would be placed in such a way as to delay the enemy and alert the main position before falling back. Security would be improved not only by patrols but by tripwires, rattles, booby-traps and illuminating flares. Cans of gasoline, ignited remotely, could provide a particularly nasty surprise, but had to be positioned sufficiently far away to silhouette the enemy without blinding or inconveniencing the defenders.

The location of automatic weapons within the defence was of primary importance, the enemy being 'expected to make every effort to locate and destroy them early in his attack. Such weapons must be moved frequently between primary, alternate, and supplementary positions, and constant care exercised to maintain deception as to their true locations. Machine guns must be protected by members of their squads armed with carbines.' Though MGs were commonly employed in pairs, it would often be desirable to employ them singly to provide 'continuous bands of interlocking fire around the position, and cover all likely avenues of approach thereto'. Although fields of fire were important, cutting of vegetation was to be kept to an absolute minimum so as not to telegraph the positions

Even such a detail as the correct grip for the machete was depicted in the US manual FM 72-20 *Jungle Warfare*, 1944. The manual recommended it both as an effective tool for cutting paths through jungle, and as 'a weapon at night when silence is imperative and firing impractical, for killing guards and sleeping enemies'. Properly used, the machete depends on its velocity rather than its weight; it is initially gripped tightly only with the thumb and first two fingers, and then snapped forward with a whipping action of the wrist – the handle is grasped firmly with the whole hand only as the blade strikes home. Cuts 'to a vine or a man's arm' were best made at an angle of about 45 degrees.

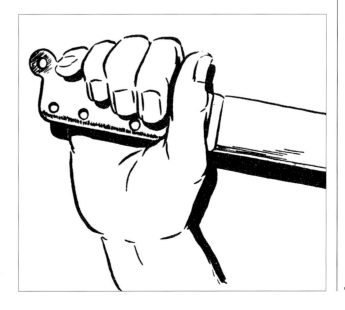

of the weapons to the enemy. Given the likely lack of observation, fire control would not be centralized at any higher than company level.

The first job of mortars and artillery was to register around the position, and to plan concentrations on given points. When decided, these concentrations would be marked on the maps of company commanders, and where they protected platoons the information would also be given to platoon commanders. For night defence fire discipline needed to be particularly strict, as uncontrolled shooting tended to disclose positions by muzzle flash. To this end the infantryman's main weapon against night attackers was the hand grenade. These were to be stored on the person, either in pockets or bandoleers, or 'on a small shelf within the emplacement, never scattered about loose in foxholes'. Where possible, enemy who infiltrated the position were to be dealt with by means of knives and bayonets, the latter to be kept fixed during the hours of darkness.

New Guinea, January 1943: after subsisting for days on pre-packed C-rations, American troops prepare a 'jungle stew' of anything and everything boiled up together. The tinned C-ration components had a fairly high calorific value, but they were never intended to keep men going for more than a very few days at a time, and failed to provide the bulk that fighting troops need. In the Pacific heat their contents often melted and separated, presenting the hungry soldier with a revolting spectacle when he opened the tin.

Patrol tactics

Patrolling was seen as vital, both to gather information and to deny it to the enemy, as well as a means of stealthy attack. Such patrols might be away from the main base for many days, and where the duration of a patrol exceeded six or seven days it was to establish a small hidden base of its own.

Of necessity, jungle patrols had to operate in column much of the time, but flank protection would be put out whenever possible 'to the limit of visibility' or a hundred yards, whichever was the closer. Jungle patrols of eight men or more were to be regarded as a 'collapsed diamond formation', which moved back into the familiar diamond shape whenever the terrain allowed. If vegetation permitted, the patrols would move off the trails entirely.

Combat patrols might vary from three men to an entire platoon, and would carry more automatic weapons and explosives as required for the mission. An emphasis on carbines over rifles was recommended, being easier to handle in thick undergrowth. An actual seven-man combat patrol led by Lt Milton Shedd on Bougainville was probably not untypical in carrying two BARs, a Thompson, a carbine, three M1 rifles and 33 grenades, and in being assisted by a native guide (see commentary, Plate F). The three-man patrol or 'scout team' was also a recognized element, usually consisting of:

'One man armed with a rifle or carbine acting as point, followed at 10 to 20 yards' distance by a second man armed with the rifle, who is in turn followed at 10 to 25 yards' by the third man armed with a light automatic weapon. All members of the three-man patrol may [instead] be armed with the submachine gun. The leading man gives his entire attention to observing the ground to the front and flanks, the second concentrates on observing for tree targets, and the third furnishes the firepower for protection of the group, and observes to the rear...

All members of the team must be constantly within visual distance of one another to afford mutual protection and control. At night, sound signals are used and distances reduced.'

TO THE LAST MAN, 1944–45

Early in the war, simple aggressive infantry tactics in jungle terrain had led to impressive Japanese victories. Standing on the defensive would lead the Japanese to their own tactical crisis. As the US Army *Handbook* observed, 'The defensive form of combat generally has been distasteful to the Japanese, and they have been reluctant to admit that the Imperial Army would ever be forced to engage in this form of combat.' In the Japanese combat regulations pertaining to the period up to 1938 there was an assumption that defence would be active – any use of fixed positions was merely to wear down the enemy until the resumption of attack. Later Japanese regulations, the *Sakusen Yomurei*, would modify this stance; but old habits died hard, and there would continue to be reckless counter-attacks, poorly co-ordinated and lacking support. Where the Allied opponents had overpowering material superiority in terms of MGs, artillery, armour, aircraft and naval gunfire support, Japanese losses were catastrophic.

Ogawa Masatsugu was actually affronted that the Australians he faced no longer wanted to have infantry battles, leaving most of the fighting to 'mechanized power'. Indeed, the bigger the battle, the less riflemen appeared to have to do with it. Under protracted machine-gun fire Ogawa no longer felt able to fire back with his bolt-action rifle, feeling 'too absurd'. Such a battle changed his 'whole way of looking at the world'.

In Burma in 1944–45, Japanese fatalities have been calculated at 13 times those of the British and Empire forces. Even where US troops had to make contested landings on islands, loss ratios could reach 10:1 or more in the Americans' favour. The willingness of the Japanese to fight to the death was universally remarked. At Gona in New Guinea Japanese wounded lying on stretchers engaged in a spirited fire-fight with the Australian troops who captured their aid post. Other wounded were quietly despatched by their own medical staff when their suffering (and the burden they represented) was judged disproportionate, or capture threatened. When all resistance was knocked out of

Plan of the Japanese defences at Buna, New Guinea, as depicted in the US *Handbook...* in October 1944. Open areas are covered by fire, but many of the bunkers and trenches are sited in woodland and jungle, and grouped for mutual support. The density of the bunker system at Cape Endaiadere is apparent. A trench dug across the old airstrip, bottom left, denies its use to the Allies.

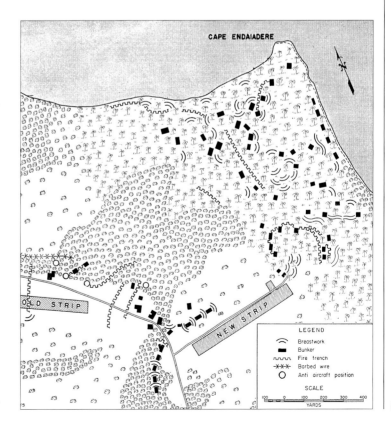

CAPE ENDAIADERE

OLD STRIP

NEW STRIP

LEGEND

⌒ Breastwork
▬ Bunker
ᴨᴨᴨ Fire trench
-x-x-x- Barbed wire
○ Anti aircraft position

SCALE
100 0   100   200   300   400
YARDS

them, some Japanese infantry simply sat quietly and waited to be killed. In other instances, when wounded or disarmed, the most spirited individuals would yell at their assailants in an attempt to frighten them off, or even try to bite them. Many kept a last grenade to end their own lives, and perhaps take one or two of the enemy with them. Lieutenant-Colonel A.S.W.Arnold recalled an occasion when his tank was confronted by a Japanese officer with a sword; when called upon to surrender, he produced a rising sun flag and stood there defiantly, until the Australian crew riddled him with machine-gun fire.

Imbalance of firepower was usually aggravated by imbalance of supply. Like the Chindits, Japanese troops ate their own horses and mules, and by the latter stages of the war eating leaves and grass in an attempt to stave off hunger was widespread. On occasion, as at the end on New Guinea, Japanese troops were reduced to eating one another. On New Britain, medic Ogawa Tamotsu recorded that 'Men killed in real combat are a very small part of those who die in war. Men died of starvation, of all kinds of disease. They just fell out one after another while on the run in the jungle [, from] amoebic dysentery, malaria, malnutrition. The ones without arms or with only one leg had to walk on their own. Worms and maggots dropped from their tattered, blood-soaked uniforms. Men suffering from dysentery walked naked.'

While Japanese tactics and logistics were failing, Allied infantry had learned an enormous amount about small unit fighting in jungle. As made clear by the diagrams in the new British manual *Warfare in the Far East* of December 1944, infiltration was now the norm. Platoons meeting resistance were to move into the jungle and around the opposition, and ambush, in many different forms, was the mainstay of defence. The 'flank' was no longer accepted as a meaningful tactical currency. On a man-to-man basis, tactical movement and aggression were expected. Advancing troops were to accept snipers as a given, looking up as well as down; 'when sniped, dive for cover. Then move quickly to a new position, locate the sniper and kill him'. If caught alone and outnumbered, men were to remain hidden and motionless. Holding fire was a recognized tactic, while 50 yards was regarded as a long shot in the jungle.

Contrary to previous instructions, grenades were not to be thrown immediately after release of the lever but at the last moment, so catching out any Japanese intent on throwing them back. *Preparation for Warfare in the Far East,* 1945, reported another grenade trick: using cup dischargers to shoot Mills bombs on 4-second fuses up into the jungle canopy, thus riddling any snipers who lurked there.

An Australian patrol advance cautiously up the so-called 'Golden Stairway' at Aitape, New Guinea, on 2 March 1945. Despite the lack of cumbersome kit plenty of ammunition is carried, and the point man has two taped magazines fitted to his Owen SMG.

* * *

A patrol of Kachins advance through the burning village of Tonnges, Burma, in December 1944. These hill tribesmen were acting in support of British 36th Div, against a settlement said to be occupied by 'Japanese police and spies'. (SEAC/ Ministry of Information SEU 1194 WPL)

Japanese tacticians saw that the prime Allied attacking method was a 'curtain of fire' that the infantry could follow. The only antidote was to attempt to split the infantry from its supporting arms with whatever weapons were available, and then counter-attack. The Allies were equipped with many automatic weapons, but fewer for hand-to-hand combat – therefore the Japanese soldier had to attempt to close with him. The tactical dilemma was summed up in a document entitled *British Army Methods and our Counter Measures,* which was captured and translated in an *Army Training Memorandum* as early as May 1943: 'Do not use passive defence if you can help it, since it has the disadvantage of making it easy for the British to build up their strong firepower. On the defensive, choose a position where the front line will not be under the enemy's fire.'

Japanese devotion to the attack, close combat and cold steel was thus never really extinguished, even though it increasingly presented itself as an irrelevance, or suicidal stupidity. The history of 26th Indian Div records an incident near Taungup, Burma, in March 1945:

'At one point the Japs had felled trees across the track for several hundred yards and were deeply entrenched with machine guns in the steep hillside. A small force of the 7th Rajput Regiment was feeling its way round the back of the hill when suddenly a Jap captain, waving a sword in his right hand and gripping a pistol in his left, leapt from a trench and ran at the company commander. Lance-Naik Bishram Singh turned his Sten gun on the officer but it jammed. The captain raised his sword to strike the Rajput officer, but before he could do so his wrist had been grabbed by Bishram Singh who in a lightning action seized the man's pistol and fired at him. As the Jap fell dead three more ran up with fixed bayonets. Bishram Singh took the pin from a grenade, ducked behind a tree, threw the grenade – and killed the lot.'

At Kangaw, the Japanese repeatedly counter-attacked over the same ground. Private Ralph of No.1 Commando described it as being 'like Rorke's Drift': 'One of our officers in 4 Troop, Lt Knowland, walked about in the open, sometimes with a 2-inch mortar… sometimes with a Bren gun, or a Tommy gun, anything he could lay his hands on… Some things stick in my mind. A Japanese Warrant Officer came charging waving his sword. Every man on the hill fired at him. Some idiot ran to

In a posed shot during follow-up operations (note the neat wooden sign, and the peacefully smoking native boatman), men of the 1st Bn Queen's Own leave an assault boat east of Waw, Burma, in 1945. In this instance the section is led by two Thompson SMGs for maximum close-range firepower. In most areas of SE Asia the road network was rudimentary, and rivers were not only natural defence lines but also the necessary highways for moving troops and supplies.

get his sword and was shot by the Japs. We dragged him back. There was a Japanese left by himself after an attack had been beaten off. He was likely to be taken prisoner, so he pulled a grenade, put it under his stomach, he was lying face down and blew himself to pieces. The enemy came within 20 yards of me. The Hill was overgrown so you couldn't see them until they got quite close. There was a Private whose name I shall not mention, who before we went into action was bragging he was going to win the VC. During the battle he hid behind a tree. There is no rhyme or reason for bravery. War is very peculiar. You get caught up in it, it is almost a game.'

On the islands of Munda and Guam, the Japanese performance was more subtle. Harassing raids were conducted mainly by night, when US Marines in foxholes might be surprised by Japanese jumping in amongst them with knives, machetes, even hatchets. Sometimes the assassin would drop into a weapons pit, stab wildly, and then spring out again. More cautious assailants would crawl forward, perhaps covered by the sound of gunfire, and roll a grenade into the American positions. Japanese would be seen fleetingly during their approach, but firing back at night carried the risk of exposure to snipers or heavy weapons which were awaiting just this opportunity. As one American corporal would put it, 'They ain't supermen; they're just tricky bastards.'

In jungle the Japanese preferred to defend high ground, but could also take advantage of the concealment of valleys. As the US *Handbook* pointed out, in jungle the concept of frontages was largely irrelevant, since small numbers were often capable of commanding the very limited avenues of approach. The Japanese habit was to establish an outpost line consisting mainly of snipers and observers, who would act as a tripwire to warn the main position. When overrun, the outpost line could fall back to the main defence; but equally, individual snipers could to ground, opening fire again into the rear of the attack, usually at the cost of their lives. Locating a sniper could be extremely difficult, even after he had fired. An account from the US 27th Div describes how skirmish lines would be pushed painstakingly through trees, men rising briefly here and there to dash forward before hitting the ground again. If a shot was fired it was answered with rapid fire from a Garand, nearby troops joining in to shoot into the same or nearby trees. When nothing happened, likely trees would still receive the occasional round.

With inadequate artillery, it became usual for Japanese gunfire to be withheld for close defence of the infantry positions, though shoots would also be organized in an attempt to silence Allied batteries. The main Japanese defence itself usually consisted of 'A series of strong points, organised in depth and mutually supporting, each one covered from the flanks and rear by riflemen in foxholes and trees. The position normally is organised for all round defence. Once the position or area to be defended has been selected, the commander plans his "fire net" or locates the positions and sectors of fire for his automatic weapons. Riflemen are disposed around these weapons... when the terrain permits, caves are utilised for the location of both automatic weapons and riflemen. Machine guns are recognised as the backbone of the defence.'

Positions were progressively improved, starting with simple 'octopus traps' and weapons pits, followed over time by the construction of bunkers, pillboxes and tunnels, until the fortifications were safe from anything except a direct hit by a large delayed action shell or bomb. Concrete was generally lacking, so local materials such as logs, earth, rice sacks and coral were substituted. Shallow communication trenches connected the bunkers and pits, and blast walls and angled entrances reduced the risks from exploding shells and enfilade fire from small arms. Camouflage was important, full advantage being taken of the quick growth of jungle plants to obtain cover. Bunker roof gradients were commonly kept as shallow as possible, to avoid casting strong shadows and to create a natural appearance.

Given the Allied preponderance in support weapons, the defenders of Japanese positions were cautioned not to open fire prematurely: optimum range was thought to be about 50 yards, or just outside grenade range. Automatic weapons would remain silent until Allied troops entered their lanes of fire and then 'annihilate the enemy before he enters the position. A heavy volume of fire is

North Borneo, May 1945: Australians of 2/43rd Inf Bn, a unit of the veteran and much-travelled 9th Div, prepare for action alongside a Matilda of 2/9th Armd Regt by netting their American SCR-506 'handie-talkie' radios to that of the tank. Effective co-operation between the two arms was one of the keys to Allied success in 1944–45, and in close jungle terrain reliable communication at the lowest levels of command was even more vital than in other theatres of war.

A failed example of the final Japanese anti-tank option – the 'human mine'. This soldier, waiting crouched in a hole dug in a jungle trail, was killed before he could die in his chosen fashion: by striking the fuse of an aerial bomb as a tank passed above him. (IWM IND 4740)

delivered at close range, and this is supplemented by grenade dischargers and mortars from positions located in the rear of the front line. Frequently, certain gun positions that are not threatened remain silent during this initial phase, only to open fire later with surprise effect. In dense jungle, observers in trees may be used to signal the automatic gunners to open fire, since the concealment of pillboxes limits visibility. Even though one or more pillboxes are neutralised, remaining automatic weapons will maintain their fire to assist counterattacking troops. Garrisons are imbued with the idea that they must fight to the last man.'

Counter-attacks could be launched to take the Allies off balance, and might be less than a section in strength led by an officer or NCO. Support weapons would commonly have registered their own positions before the arrival of an Allied attack, and the Japanese had no scruple in battering friendly positions where it was calculated that the enemy might suffer the greater loss.

Tank/infantry co-operation

Conversely, Allied infantry learned new methods to deal with strongpoints. In early January 1943 the Australians were already combining tanks with *ad hoc* demolition squads. The tanks would batter the position, clearing any enemy who appeared on the surface with HE and machine-gun fire. The first infantry team would then shove a powerful improvised charge through the nearest bunker opening. Once this had exploded a second team would come up and throw cans of petrol inside which would then be ignited by tracer rounds or flares.

A few months later the US Marines were using dedicated 'assault demolition teams' – commonly two such teams, of platoon strength, per regiment, based on either a flame-thrower or a light machine gun. Experience on Peleliu in September 1944 also led to the evolution of what became known as 'pin up' tactics. A team comprising a bazooka, two BARs and a rifleman would saturate the enemy position with fire: with the defenders effectively pinned, other teams could advance to deal with the bunker at point blank range. Demolition squads would use either a satchel charge or a bangalore torpedo, while flame-thrower teams would have a pair of man-pack weapons, protected as they went forward by two riflemen. Such techniques became known as the 'corkscrew and blowtorch method', and later formed part of USMC training.

A factor which seriously hampered Japanese defence was the lack of good anti-tank guns; the basic 37mm Type 94 gun was only capable of penetrating an inch of armour at 1,000 yards. Umeo Tokita of the

215th Infantry witnessed the brave but futile effort of one gun in Burma: 'The crew of a 37mm anti-tank gun pushed up the gun and its first shot pierced a tank's track but that was all. No more shells penetrated the armour. Most of our gunners were killed by the concentrated fire from tanks, and the gun itself was run over by a tank and smashed.' The 47mm Type 01 which arrived in 1942 could pierce two inches at 500 yards; though this was effective against light tanks, it could only knock out the standard Allied tank, the M4 Medium (Sherman) with a hull or turret shot at very close range. The Japanese compensated for its mediocre performance by skilful concealment and holding fire until the last moment. Armour-piercing ammunition was produced for a variety of other pieces including field and infantry guns; AT rifles and rifle-grenades were widely used, but with disappointing results.

The Japanese theory of infantry anti-tank defence was described as *dansei bogyo* or 'elastic'. According to the textbook, upon receiving a major tank attack some of the infantry were to fall back within the position while a specially trained platoon from each company engaged the armour, mainly with smoke grenades and anti-tank mines, and preferably on ground – such as narrow trails through forest – where tanks were slow and vulnerable. Fortunately for many Allied tank crews, Japanese AT munitions seldom matched the bravery of the men who used them. Anti-tank mines were placed by men crawling in front of

A classic shot from the final victorious advances in Burma: CSM Watkins and Pte Lavell, 6th Bn South Wales Borderers, passing the Bahe Pagoda during a patrol following the capture of this Burmese village by 71st Indian Inf Bde, 36th Div, in summer 1945. The 6th SWB, who took over from the 1st Lincolns as the single British battalion in this Indian brigade, had actually been trained as tank crews in Britain earlier in the war – a reminder that any wartime Tommy might be set to any task and sent to any battle front. In this case the battalion probably still had many men who understood the limitations of vision from inside tanks, with positive consequences for the unit's co-operation with armour in the attack.

tanks, or drawing mines across tracks on cords from concealed foxholes – both last-minute and virtually suicidal tactics. For the absolutely suicidal, swarming charges were made against the tanks on foot, culminating with blinding the crew's vision apertures and using Molotov cocktails, hand-placed magnetic charges, or even wooden beams, picks and pistols against tracks and hatches respectively in attempts to immobilize the tank and get a grenade inside. The 'lunge' mine, a shaped charge on the end of a two-metre pole, detonated when it was thrust against the tank. Allied tank crews in turn improvised various security measures, and often 'hosed down' each other's tanks with point-blank MG fire.

* * *

By the end of the war, mastery of jungle fighting had moved decisively in favour of the Allies. This was partly a matter of firepower and logistics, but equally a function of mental attitude and the detail of infantry tactics. As *Warfare in the Far East* put it:

'It goes without saying that the men who fight in the jungle must be well trained and well led and must be jungle minded. They must move in single file, but must be ready at all times to deploy and drop noiselessly out of sight. Every man must be capable, if the need arises, of acting as an individual and being able to support himself. Officers should be fitter and more alert than their men; able to interest them and train them in the craft of the jungles in which they are to fight. Jungle warfare should be regarded as a game, healthful [!], interesting, and thrilling; the men should feel at home in the jungle. They must realize the absolute necessity for jungle training as a means to defeat the Japanese, who come from one of the most highly industrialized countries in the world and have no natural advantages as jungle infantry.'

PLATE COMMENTARIES

A: IMPROVEMENTS IN JUNGLE UNIFORMS & EQUIPMENT

A1: Lance-corporal, Vickers MMG No.1, 1st Battalion Manchester Regiment; Singapore, October 1941

The 1st Manchesters were converted to a Machine Gun Battalion in 1937, and arrived in Singapore the following year. When other battalions of the Singapore garrison were moved north on to the Malayan mainland an extra 'R' Company was formed by 1st Manchesters, consisting of one MG and three rifle platoons. Using all the battalion transport and eight hired Chinese lorries, its mission was to prevent breakthroughs and to counter enemy tanks. The uniform of this No.1 of a Vickers crew – here carrying the Mk IV tripod, as per standard operating procedure – is based on a photo in the Manchesters' regimental history, and is a good example of how a British soldier in the tropics was expected to look at the outbreak of war with Japan. This is supposed to be combat uniform, although the general impression is one of peacetime smartness and precision.

The old Wolseley sun helmet displays the battalion flash of a dark green tilted square with the gilt fleur-de-lys regimental badge, and a lemon-yellow top fold to the *paggri*. The addition of a few leaves makes for laughably ineffective camouflage. A single white tape rank chevron is temporarily attached to the right sleeve. The khaki cotton aertex shirt and khaki drill shorts were designed for the parched hills of India,

not for the jungle; the colour is highly visible against a green background, and the short sleeves and legs invite mosquito bites and thorn scratches, leading to malaria and festering sores and ulcers. His 37 Pattern webbing equipment includes the pistol set for machine gunners, and he wears the gasmask satchel in the 'ready' position on his chest.

The reliable Vickers .303in MMG was one of the largest weapons to see regular jungle use, since it could be broken down into mule loads. Full use of the effective range of 3,000 yards was rarely achievable due to the lack of fields of observation and fire in forested terrain.

A2: US Marine, 2nd Marine Raider Battalion; Bougainville, November 1943

Four Marine Raider battalions were formed from January 1942. They carried out a number of daring operations on Japanese-held islands, and their last (before being disbanded, and absorbed into a reborn 4th Marine Regt in February 1944) was the opening stage of the recapture of Bougainville in November 1943. In appearance and firepower this man has made considerable strides since 1941, when the US Army and Marines were outfitted as unsuitably for jungle fighting as were the British.

The USMC P1942 two-piece jungle suit was reversible from this 'green' side to a 'brown' side (though this was seldom exposed in practice); its use sharply diminished in 1944 among Marine rifle units, who found it to be too visible in many types of terrain. Here the Raider wears the plain sage-green utility 'cover' and carries his M1 helmet slung at his belt. His boots are standard russet leather 'rough-out' field shoes. His web equipment – '782 gear' – includes a M1936 pistol belt supported by the suspenders of the USMC's special M1941 pack system, here worn in Field Marching Order with the haversack only, around which is strapped the rolled reversible camouflage poncho. His main weapon is a .45cal M1928A1 Thompson sub-machine gun with the early 50-round drum magazine – heavy, but prized for its sustained firepower. He has one spare drum in a slung pouch, but also 30-round box magazines in a triple belt pouch under it on his right hip. The M1911A1 semi-automatic pistol in the same calibre is holstered in front of this, with a double pouch for spare clips on the left of the belt. Finally, he carries the big Collins No.18 'machete' with a blade nearly 10in long; this bush- and fighting-knife was christened the 'Gung Ho' by the 2nd Bn CO, LtCol Evans Carlson, who had it issued to his unit in September/October 1942. The rear of the pack and belt would support an entrenching shovel, two waterbottles, and perhaps wirecutters.

A3: Able Seaman, Royal Australian Navy Commandos; Queensland, Australia, September 1944

Based on a photo of AB E.G.Cargill taken at Trinity Beach during jungle warfare training, this figure wears the felt slouch hat with the brim down all round, and a short section

Drinking water was needed in large quantities in the Far East; here Sepoy Hali Ram of 19th Indian Div takes a drink from his *chagul* or water bag. His tropical-weight green battledress and 37 Pattern web equipment would all have been made in India. Like most infantry in the front line, he carries an additional 50-round disposable bandolier for his .303in SMLE rifle. (IWM IND4483)

of the RAN cap tally – 'H.M.A.S.' – sewn to the right side. The hat was relatively costly, and did not stand up well to the constant damp of the jungle, but was usually retained out of national pride; attempts to replace it with a lightweight jungle-green beret were unpopular. The shirt and trousers of rot-proofed materials in varying shades of green were adopted in 1943, replacing earlier green-dyed khaki drill items; the US canvas leggings were worn with rot-proofed Australian boots with special jungle studs on the soles.

His webbing equipment is basically the British 37 Ptn set with 'jungle' modifications including wider basic pouches, apart from the Australian 'long range patrol' pack. Probably devised in 1942 and officially recommended early in 1943 following experience in New Guinea, this used the waterproofed groundsheet/rain poncho. Spare clothing, rations and washing kit were laid on the groundsheet, which was rolled up and arranged in an M-shape, held in place with two horizontal pack straps from the 08 large pack; it was then attached to the L-shaped shoulder straps of the 37 small pack. This was superior for jungle use to the various field modifications of the 08 and 37 packs made by some other units, for lack of a practical jungle rucksack. This commando is armed with the Australian-made .303in SMLE No.1 Mk III* rifle, and has an Australian 1944 machete at his hip.

B: JAPANESE COMBINED ARMS 'SPECIAL TACTICS', 1941–42
Colonel Masanobu Tsuji's 'special tactics' for seizing defended bridges on a narrow front, as for example in the jungles of Malaya in 1941–42. The forward parties of infantry cross the river using seized native boats, under cover of darkness or rain; they then take up skirmishing positions on the south bank to cover the engineers who repair the demolished bridge (A). The Japanese artillery concentrates on the British artillery guarding bridge (B), neutralizing its ability to interfere with this work. As soon as the repair is completed the Japanese force attacks, preferably by night, with infantry outflanking the British defence while the tanks and reserves punch down the road. They advance rapidly to the next river line before bridge (B) can be destroyed.

C: JAPANESE NIGHT ATTACK, 1943
Although based on a specific attack by a section of the 112th Inf Regt, 55th Div, at Horseshoe Hill, Burma, in April 1943, the basic elements shown were in use throughout the war, and could be used up to company level. These tactics were suitable for plantations, broken ground and scrub, but not for the densest secondary jungle.

C1: The section of 10–12 men advance up a grassy slope and into fairly open jungle, spaced out in a rough single file with each man separated from the next by about 8–10 feet. These intervals will reduce the effect of enemy fire and allow the best use of fieldcraft, while being short enough for each man to keep in sight the white patch displayed on the back of the next man's helmet. The NCO section leader is at the head of the column. The rifles are carried with loaded magazines and fixed bayonets, but not with a round in the breech – except in an emergency, the intention is that the attackers will get amongst the defenders with the bayonet. The men have been given a password and reply – for instance, *fakuro/ nazumi* ('bag/rat') – for use in case they get separated in the darkness.

Bren gun 'tree mounting', enabling LMG fire over undergrowth – from the British manual *Forest, Bush and Jungle Warfare*, 1942.

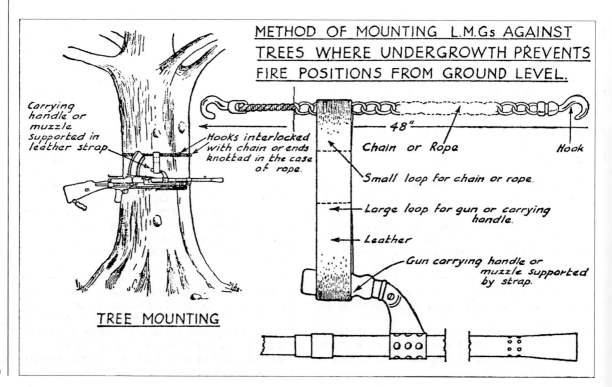

METHOD OF MOUNTING L.M.Gs AGAINST TREES WHERE UNDERGROWTH PREVENTS FIRE POSITIONS FROM GROUND LEVEL.

Carrying handle or muzzle supported in leather strap

Hooks interlocked with chain or ends knotted in the case of rope.

Chain or Rope

Hook

— 48" —

Small loop for chain or rope.

Large loop for gun or carrying handle.

Leather

Gun carrying handle or muzzle supported by strap.

TREE MOUNTING

C2: At about 100 yards from the enemy positions the section leader halts and extends his arms. At this signal his men move silently from column into a loose skirmish line, and drop to the ground, continuing the advance at a crawl. Although the enemy may now realize that they are being approached, and may open fire blindly, the attackers continue to crawl forward, taking advantage of the uneven ground; most enemy fire will pass above them, and since the attack is up a slope they present no silhouettes against the sky.

C3: When they are within a few feet of the enemy position the section leader yells 'Charge!', and every man rises to his feet and rushes forwards simultaneously. In the dark, the multiple target they present is too fleeting for many to receive aimed fire before they are mingling with the defenders. Any reinforcements or flank attacks by other troops will now be unleashed, while the defenders are confused and preoccupied by the frontal attack. Depending upon the situation and prior orders, the section may occupy the captured position, or move on a short distance before digging in – to avoid the danger of the enemy shelling their own abandoned position.

C4: Japanese infantryman in night attack order

He wears conventional Type 98 khaki tropical shirt and trousers with wool puttees, and brown leather equipment carrying 120 rounds for his 6.5mm Arisaka Type 38 rifle. The Type 90 steel helmet is worn with a khaki cotton drawstring cover, to the rear of which is sewn a white nighttime recognition patch about 4in square. He has dropped his pack and haversack; his leather hobnail boots are muffled with strips of hessian (burlap), as is the scabbard of his bayonet to stop it rattling against his slung canteen. The bayonet itself is dulled with mud to prevent reflections, and he has smeared soot from a cookpot on his face and hands.

D: AUSTRALIAN SECTION TACTICS, 1943

Drawn from Australian 6th Div instructions of July 1943, these four diagrams illustrate likely section deployments in jungle conditions.

D1: Section advancing on jungle track

In the scout group, the 'forward scout' leads the 'second scout' by about 5 yards, and the 'connecting file' is close behind the second scout. After another 4- or 5-yard gap, the section leader leads the gun (LMG) group, but can 'float' between the groups at need; the other three men of the group maintain intervals of about a yard. Behind the gun group 'No.3', another 4- or 5-yard gap is left open before the support group, who are also spaced at roughly one-yard intervals.

D2: Section deployment upon contact

The gun group 'Nos.1 & 2' take up prone firing positions to the front, with 'No.3' to the rear, ready to give them covering fire or bring up more magazines. The flank scouts lie down behind cover 5 or 6 yards to left and right. The section leader kneels in the centre, controlling the action. About 10 yards behind and left of the LMG, the support group stand or kneel in all-round defence, ready to move up on either flank as ordered.

D3: Section deployment for penetration

The scout group are spaced out by a yard or two, one rifleman prone and the second and the SMG gunner kneeling to his rear. The section leader is central, another couple of yards behind. The LMG and two riflemen are spaced out about 10 yards back and to one side, standing facing the flank and ready to move forward past the scouts if ordered. The support group are in all-round defence behind the other flank.

D4: Section holding position

The section are holding ground after contact, in readiness for further action; all are in prone firing positions, except the section commander, who remains kneeling, ready to observe and move in any direction. The sentry group are concealed from most directions; one of the scouts – the 'getaway man' – runs 10 yards back to report a sighting to the section leader. The gun group, spaced at yard intervals in a rough triangle, face forwards. Behind them the support group, spaced a couple of yards apart, form a rough crescent, covering the flanks and rear.

E: AUSTRALIAN SECTION DEFENSIVE POSITIONS, 1943

These are again based upon diagrams in the tactical manual of the veteran 6th Div, whose brigades returned from the Middle East to fight in New Guinea in 1942, and continued to do so until final victory in 1945.

E1: General view of a section position

This shows the layout of a dug-in position placed in the edge of thick jungle, to cover open jungle or elephant grass beyond a stream (which will slow any attack from that direction). It is part of a larger defensive scheme and enjoys protective MMG fire from a flank; but this cannot cover the whole front, and the section LMG is placed so as to command the approaches through open jungle or grassland, while rifles, SMGs and grenades protect the flank and rear approaches through thick forest. A sentry post, initially manned by a sniper covered by an SMG man, is placed a little way upstream, with good fields of fire both up and down the stream bed; if a threat appears the sentries may decide to open fire, moving from position to position, or simply to fall back on the rest of the section. The accompanying text to the original diagrams mentions dummy posts, not dug in but indicated by deliberate surface disturbance (and perhaps discarded ammo boxes, etc), to draw attackers into fields of fire.

E2: Detail view of a section position

This is a typical example of a well-prepared, dug-in position from the 6th Division manual, but there was nothing uniform about such positions; concealment and fields of fire took priority. It is about 45–50ft across, with four main weapons pits **(A, C, D and E)** about 6ft × 3ft, each for two men. The LMG **(A, and inset detail)** commands one or more long fields of fire; the rifles and SMG men **(C, D & E, and inset detail)** are positioned to face points where the enemy may make a short rush. The section commander is at **(B)**. All these open positions are linked by crawl trenches with overhead camouflage; the weapon pits have no sandbags or spoil at the parapets, for the sake of concealment. At various points along the trenches, shelters **(rectangles, and inset detail)**, and caches for ammunition and rations **(squares)**, have camouflaged water- and splinter-proof roofs made from two layers of logs sandwiching at least 9in of earth, preferably in ammo boxes, etc. To avoid movement above ground, there is even a pre-dug latrine pit **(L)** at the end of a trench.

F: US ARMY PATROL, BOUGAINVILLE, 1944

This illustration is based on the memories of Lts Milton Shedd and Charles H.Walker of Co E, 164th Inf, 23rd 'Americal' Div, quoted in the latter's memoir *Combat Officer*. It shows a seven-man patrol, plus a Solomons Islander guide **(1)**, approaching a suspected contact; photos of native guides often show them as naked apart from a 'kilt' (lap-lap) and basic US web equipment, and armed with the M1903 bolt-action rifle. The patrol commander **(2)** has just closed up on the lead scout, and motions one of his two BAR gunners and a covering rifleman **(4 & 5)** forward out of single file and on to the right flank; when the vegetation allows, the other men – a Thompson gunner **(3)**, the second BAR man **(6)** and two more riflemen **(7 & 8)** – will also work their way forward to shake out into a skirmish line for the final advance to contact. Unknown to them, they are about to stumble on a

Kelanoa, New Guinea, 1944: Cpl Sala, MM, of A Coy, 1st Papuan Inf Bn, photographed cradling his 9mm Owen SMG. The locally recruited 1st Papuans, with their impressive jungle-craft, were a very useful adjunct to the Australian forces; Cpl Sala was awarded the Military Medal after being credited with the elimination of 36 of the enemy. The Owen's top-mounted magazine gave gravity-assisted feed, and the gun had good sealing against dirt, but it was also comparatively heavy and had a violent action.

Japanese rifleman waiting concealed in an 'octopus trap' **(detail J)** or 'spider hole'. Improved versions of these might have a cubby-hole for kit dug into the wall.

The 164th Inf was originally a North Dakota National Guard unit, but replacements came from all over the USA and even included numbers of Mexicans from south of the border. The patrol members wear M1 helmets, olive drab M1942 or M1943 herringbone twill fatigues (HBTs), and standard web gear. The useful jungle pack **(detail 8)** appeared in 1943 but remained a 'limited standard' issue. Each man carried his blanket and poncho in the pack, with such items as a small mosquito head-net, rations for the seven- to ten-day patrol, and at least one in every six men a Coleman gasoline cooker; some carried TNT blocks with fuse and detonators, for creating instant foxholes and booby-traps; and if a 60mm mortar was taken along then each man had to carry some of its bombs. Here the T-handled entrenching spade and a machete are stowed on the pack.

The rifle ammo belt included full clips each of tracer, armour-piercing and incendiary rounds, each always being kept in the same pouches. Each man carried three canteens – two with water and one with fuel for the cooker; a fighting knife; and a jungle first aid kit with the smaller Carlisle pack hooked beneath it. There was no issue of camouflage cream, and at one time Easy Company made do with gentian-purple ointment from the medical officer (detail 6). The patrol carried 33 grenades between them; when he could, Walker traded with a British Empire unit for No.36 'Mills bombs', preferred for their more lethal fragmentation. This US regiment also set up a jungle tracking school with instructors borrowed from the 3rd Fijian Bn, who could trace by smell alone which leaves had been touched by a man's hands.

G: BRITISH 'ADVANCE ON A BROAD FRONT'; BURMA, 1944–45

G1: The tactical diagram is copied from the British manual *Warfare in the Far East* of December 1944. It shows how platoons and companies are supposed to advance through enemy-held positions in jungle and scrub, rather than attacking them directly. The key point is that there is no continuous 'front': British tactics have developed to copy Japanese infiltration techniques. The Japanese hold key points on the tracks and in the villages; but though some of these are engaged, the majority of the attacking force bypasses them, going on to seize the vital village that blocks all the tracks, the railway and the main river bridge. Being outflanked or surrounded are no longer the make-or-break issues that they were in 1941/42; nor are the British forces dependent on crowded road columns which the Japanese might ambush or strike from the air. They now have years of experience in fighting the Japanese in all types of terrain; plentiful and superior tanks and air cover; and sufficient riverboats for parallel advances.

G2: Private, 1st Battalion Essex Regiment; Operation 'Thursday', February 1944

This Chindit infantryman is equipped for a local patrol from his column's perimeter. He wears the felt bush hat based on the Australian model, an Indian-made shirt and lightweight denim battledress trousers in jungle-green, 'ammo boots' and wool ankle puttees. His equipment is limited to a disposable cotton bandolier for ten rifle clips tied around his waist, his SMLE rifle, and a machete. The long bayonet was awkward in close country, and normally was not fixed unless contact was imminent.

G3: Private, 1st Battalion Worcestershire Regiment; Irrawaddy River, Burma, May 1945

This soldier from the British unit of 29 Indian Inf Bde is dressed entirely in Indian-made clothing and equipment: the lightweight jungle-green battledress blouse and trousers, the new short-brimmed cloth jungle hat that was just beginning to reach British troops, and Indian-made 37 Ptn webbing Fighting Order. His weapon is also new: the Rifle No.5 or 'jungle carbine', a shortened version of the No.4 (39in from 44in); although handier in thick country, and 1.6lb lighter, it was not popular. The shorter barrel needed a flash-hider at the muzzle, and the lighter weight gave it an even harder recoil 'kick' than the full-length .303in rifles despite a rubber shoulder pad. Troops in the jungle were sometimes ordered to leave the slings off their rifles, to ensure that they were carried ready for instant action at all times.

H: AMBUSH TECHNIQUES

In jungle country the reduced visibility and the relative difficulty of using support fire weapons made ambushes a critical element of infantry tactics. This plate shows four ambush tactics in a single imaginary landscape.

H1: Japanese road ambush, 1944

This is based on a US manual of 1944. A roadblock has been placed just round a corner from the Allied direction of advance. A camouflaged anti-tank gun has been positioned to fire down the length of the approach road. Infantry occupy positions in the fringe of the jungle on both sides of the bend, with fields of fire in both directions and thus able to fire on the head, flank and tail of the Allied column and to protect the AT gun from a rush. When no AT gun was available, machine guns or AT rifles might be used instead.

H2: Australian ambush at stream crossing, 1943

A scheme from the Australian 6th Div manual shows how as few as two men could set an ambush and hope to escape. At a creek crossing, one man takes position to have a view of any enemy approaching the ford, and to fire along the length of the stream into their flank; a second is placed to fire straight down the track towards the water; both are well concealed, and their fire intersects at the crossing point. After doing as much damage as they can, then either at a pre-arranged signal or when they come under fire themselves, both abandon their posts and make their way back to the rendezvous by separate routes.

H3: British platoon 'quick ambush', 1944

Based on a scheme from *Warfare in the Far East*, 1944. Again, a roadblock has been placed just around a bend from the enemy direction of advance, with the object of annihilating a Japanese force of similar strength. Most of the British platoon take position back from the road with their rifles and SMGs, in two separate groups on either side of the road but not overlapping, so as to avoid 'friendly fire' casualties. When the ambush is sprung the *piéce de résistance* is the use of the platoon's Bren guns, whose teams dash out on to the road behind the enemy and fire straight down it to catch them in a crossfire from three directions. As the enemy fall or become confused the ambush groups close in from both sides for the final kill.

H4: British multi-platoon ambush, 1944

Published in the same manual, this scheme was in fact taken from Chindit tactics; it shows how several platoons can use their LMGs and 2in mortars in concert to attack a substantial column on a bend. The mortars are positioned some distance away with the range to the road preregistered. The LMGs are positioned well back from the edge, but in positions which give good fields of fire along the road in both directions, taking advantage of the bends and straights. Rifles and SMGs are placed close to the road but on one side only. As the head of the enemy column begins to emerge from the bend the mortars and LMGs open fire; most of the enemy have no obvious way to react, being bracketed by mortar bombs and swept by machine-gun fire from front and rear. Some are sniped by riflemen as they leave their vehicles; others are shot down at close range as they try to dive off the road into cover. In the event of failure, or at a pre-arranged signal, the ambush parties withdraw to a rendezvous, their retreat covered by the LMGs, and from this RV they march for their more distant base.

INDEX

References to illustrations are shown in **bold**.
Plates are shown with page and caption
locators in brackets.